Uplies
Hurstperpoint
Blackb.
New Close
E
Albourne
W. Town
Albourne place
Keymer
Cross
Wickham 6
Streete
Dany 21
Ditchling
Ashurst
Newtimber Place
Wolstonbury hill
Clayton
Westmiston
Fulling mill
Wales
90
Newtimber
HUND.
Piecombe
Plumpton
Poyning
OF
Pangdean
Ditchling Cast. hill
olking
Sadlescomb
Poormans Wall
35
Standean
Part of Ringmer
Hundred
in Deanries Malling
POYNINGS
W
Stammer
Borne
HUND.
E
OF FISHERS
Hangleton
Stammer Crofs
GATE
HUND
Patcham
Falmer
Patcham Windmill
Hollingbury
Blatchington
OF
DEANE
HUNDRED
Whiteing
Portslade
Moulecomt
Hadshurfe
OF
HUND
Preston 135
Portslade gap
OF
Preston place
Ruins of Aldrington &
PRESTON
Hove
HUND. OF
YOUUSMERE
Parfonage
WHALESB=
ONE
Brighthelmston
Ovingdean
It appears by an Infcription
at hove parfonage that fince
y year 1099 y Sea has gained
in that is aft 6 Perches.
Black
Ron

Bygone
STEYNING
BRAMBER
and
BEEDING

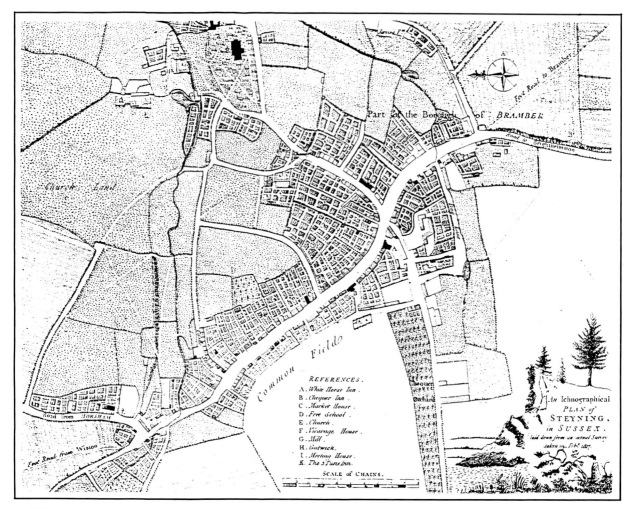

REFERENCES.

A. White Horse Inn.
B. Chequer Inn.
C. Market House.
D. Free School.
E. Church.
F. Vicarage House.
G. Mill.
H. Gatwick.
I. Meeting House.
K. The 3 Tuns Inn.

SCALE of CHAINS.

An Ichnographical PLAN of STEYNING, in SUSSEX. laid down from an actual Survey taken in Feb.y 1817.

   This map drawn in 1817 shows the centre of Steyning little altered today; both *White Horse Inn* and the *Chequer Inn* are still in existence. Church Street adjoins the High Street and the building known as Brotherhood Hall, now part of Steyning Grammar School, is shown as (D) Free School. It is interesting to note that a certain area of the town is in the Borough of Bramber.

Bygone
STEYNING
BRAMBER
and
BEEDING

Aylwin Guilmant

Phillimore

1988

Published by
PHILLIMORE & CO. LTD.
Shopwyke Hall, Chichester, Sussex

ISBN 0 85033 669 4

Printed and bound by
BIDDLES LTD.
Guildford, Surrey

*This book is dedicated to the people of
Steyning, Bramber and Beeding, both past and present,
among them my two grand-daughters, Morguana and Keridwen,
who are growing up in this delightful locality*

This book is a tribute to all the people of Steyning, Bramber and Beeding who have given their time to me and who have loaned me their photographs from their family collections

List of Illustrations

Frontispiece: Map of the centre of Steyning, 1817
Endpapers: A section of Richard Budgen's map of Sussex, 1724

1. 19th-century drawing of St Andrew's church
2. Steyning church and vicarage in 1781
3. Drawing of St Andrew's nave, dated 1780
4. St Andrew's lychgate, *c*.1904
5. William Cowerson's tombstone in St Andrew's churchyard
6. The tithe barn
7. Interior of St Andrew's church
8. A copy of the Charter signed by William the Conqueror
9. Stone gargoyle
10. Carved panels depicting the life of St Cuthman
11. 'Penn's House', the Quaker meeting place
12. High Street, Steyning, *c*.1900
13. Steyning water pump early this century
14. Steyning High Street, pre-1914
15. Outside the *Chequer Inn*, *c*.1920
16. High Street looking south-west
17. Carved beam in Steyning post office
18. An artist's impression of Church Street, *c*.1800
19. Church Street, *c*.1860
20. Children in Church Street, *c*.1900
21. 15th-century building used as the workhouse
22. The Stone House
23. Coin minted in Steyning in the reign of King William I
24. Old cottage in Church Side
25. Shoes found hidden in the eaves of a local house
26. A school group, *c*.1883
27. Mr. and Mrs. George Burgess Michell, *c*.1895
28. Kenneth, Eric and Noel Michell, *c*.1890
29. & 30. Charles Stewart Parnell and Katherine O'Shea
31. The circle of beech trees at Chanctonbury Ring
32. Wiston House, home of the Goring family
33. Children in Elm Grove early this century
34. Albert Coote, aged 99 years
35. Lithograph of Gatewick house, *c*.1860
36. The pond of Court Mill, *c*.1906
37. Drawing of the mill-wheel at Court Mill, 1926
38. A painting of the cattle market in Church Street, 1890
39. Cattle market in the High Street, *c*.1890
40. The Fat Stock Show of 1930
41. Steyning Young Farmers' Club, *c*.1932
42. A horse sale in Steyning, 1937
43. Lambs at Steyning Fat Stock Show, *c*.1930
44. Poster advertising a Gift Sale in aid of the Royal Agricultural Benevolent Institution
45. Loading potatoes on Cross's Farm, *c*.1932
46. Sheep yards or standing folds on the South Downs
47. The post office, before 1920
48. Mr. F. Seymour's greengrocery, High Street, *c*.1936
49. Mr. Lewis Wood as a toddler, *c*.1910
50. Mr. Wood senior with three new cars outside his showroom
51. The International Stores, *c*.1910
52. Steyning policemen outside their station
53. The fire station
54. Steyning fire brigade in 1910
55. P. Oliver, fire chief at Steyning, *c*.1906
56. Steyning fire brigade in action
57. Steyning's first motor fire engine, *c*.1924
58. A sketch of the Old Malthouse, Chantry Green, 1890
59. The southern end of the High Street, *c*.1905
60. Gates' Brewery plant
61. A painting of Church Street, *c*.1860
62. Tweed Brothers' Forge in Church Street, *c*.1920
63. The Tweed brothers, Fred and Horace
64. Charles Woolgar outside the wheelwright works in School Lane
65. Two types of cart produced by the Woolgar family
66. F. Duke, Ltd., builders, decorators and timber merchants, *c*.1930
67. Saw-pit in operation, before World War One
68. Premises of J. Wood, Butcher, *c*.1910
69. Wood's family butchers in the High Street, *c*.1915
70. The *White Horse*, *c*.1900
71. A facsimile of a poster advertising coaching to London
72. Railway employees
73. The railway station, built by Mr. Chappell, *c*.1860
74. Train ticket, 1966

75. A peaceful scene at Steyning cricket ground, June 1914
76. A tug-of-war in the recreation ground in 1910
77. Fête in the early 1900s
78. Steyning football club, 1907-8
79. The Crawley and Horsham hunt at Steyning
80. Horace Green, the winner of the walking race on 6 May 1903
81. Programme of Steyning and District Annual Walking Races, April 1925
82. An early photograph of the walking race
83. The 'line-up' for the younger boys, 1938
84. Cavalry in Sheep Pen Lane, Steyning, c.1910
85. Brotherwood Hall decked with bunting in 1919
86. Peace celebration in Steyning, 1919
87. Armistice Service on 15 November 1925
88. The 209th Field Company Royal Engineers, July 1939
89. No. 3 Steyning Section of the Royal Engineers, 1939
90. Air raid precaution exercise during World War Two
91. V-Day celebrations at Steyning
92. Celebrations for Queen Victoria's Golden Jubilee in 1887
93. Friendly Societies procession
94. Procession in memory of King Edward VII
95. Outside the *George Inn*, on a day of national mourning
96. An inter-denominational memorial service in honour of King Edward VII
97. Filming in Church Street, 1924
98. Carnival at Steyning, 1929
99. A bird's-eye view of Bramber village, c.1920
100. The ruined church of St Nicholas at Bramber, 1785
101. Drawing of St Nicholas's church, c.1850
102. Reconstruction of Bramber Castle in the Norman period
103. The surviving wall of the keep, c.1900
104. Children in a waggonette in the grounds of the castle
105. Drawing of Bramber bridge
106. Bridge crossing the Adur at Beeding
107. St Mary's, c.1860
108. St Mary's, when run as a farm, c.1860
109. St Mary's early this century
110. The music room added to St Mary's in 1896
111. Canadian troops stationed at St Mary's in 1941
112. An early print of Bramber village, c.1840
113. Early photograph of Bramber village, c.1865
114. Painting of the toll-gate at Bramber, c.1860
115. An early tub race on the flooded road
116. *Castle Hotel*, 1904
117. Flooded road, 1911
118. Bramber village during the floods of 1924-5
119. Delivery of provisions by boat in the floods of 1925
120. Mr. Potter outside his Museum of Curiosity at Bramber
121. Bramber High Street, c.1900
122. The River Adur, c.1905
123. A tea garden, Bramber, c.1925
124. A horse being shod, c.1908
125. Bramber High Street, looking east, c.1920
126. Beeding Priory House
127. Beeding village street in 1905
128. Infants and teacher outside Beeding school, c.1890
129. Beeding school-house
130. Upper Beeding schoolchildren in 1919
131. A class at Beeding school, c.1930
132. Beeding Scout and Cub troop, c.1920
133. Some boys of Beeding earlier this century
134. Beeding trap ball team
135. The post mill, c.1870
136. Notice of sale of the post mill, Upper Beeding
137. Drawing of the Upper Beeding windmill, c.1860
138. A. J. Perry's delivery cart, c.1920
139. Pre-1913 Humber delivery van
140. Beeding High Street, c.1915
141. Beeding postmistress and her brother outside 'Holly cottage'
142. Riverside, Upper Beeding
143. Blue Circle Industries PLC
144. Cement barges on the River Adur, early this century
145. Beeding men building 'Dacre Villas'
146. The *Rising Sun*, Upper Beeding
147. George Bazen shearing sheep at Hoe Court Farm
148. Mr. and Mrs. Cross, moving from Somerset to Beeding Court Farm
149. Beeding Court, c.1905
150. George Bailey, shepherd at Beeding Court Farm
151. The Towers, Upper Beeding, c.1870
152. Nuns from the convent of the Blessed Sacrament, 1909
153. The 'family' at The Towers, c.1885
154. The servants at The Towers
155. Beeding and Bramber Infant Welfare Clinic in 1930
156. A wedding at St Peter's church, 1909
157. Beeding and Bramber flower show, 1913
158. 'Buns and treacle' event at the fête, 1927
159. Bramber and Beeding fête, 1927
160. Children's fancy dress, 1927
161. Bramber and Beeding Women's Institute anniversary party, 1928
162. Char-a-banc outside the *Bridge Inn*, 1921

Acknowledgements

David Arscott, Esq. (BBC Radio Sussex); Mr. and Mrs. T. Ashdown; Beeding and Bramber Local History Society; Blue Circle Industries PLC Beeding, the Works Manager; Mrs. Marjorie Boyd; Brighton Central Reference Library, the Chief Librarian; The British Library; The British Museum; Rev. Peter Burch; Rev. B. Coote; Ian Dean (Director Chalk Pits Museum, Industrial History Centre, Amberley); Mrs. Diana Durden; Mrs. Ruby Edmonds; Miss O. Elms; Mrs. Gillian Fox; Barry Funnell, Esq.; Mr. and Mrs. Colin Garfield; Mrs. D. Garratt; Paul Gelder (Editor, *The West Sussex Gazette*); Mrs. Patricia Gill (County Archivist, West Sussex Record Office); R. H. Goring (The Wiston Estate); J. S. Gray; John Green; Mrs. Joan Ham; Mrs. G. Hooker (Headmistress, Upper Beeding Primary School); Dr. Tim Hudson (Victoria County History); R. J. Huse (the County Librarian, West Sussex); Mr. and Mrs. Aubrey Isaacs; Mr. and Mrs. Gordon Jones; Ms. Elizabeth Kelly (Curator, Horsham Museum); Dr. Richard Marks (Curator, Brighton Museum); Tony Mayes (Editor, *Worthing Guardian*); John Montgomery; National Library of Ireland; Keith Nethercoate-Bryant; John Norwood (Curator, Worthing Museum); Leslie Oppitz; Mrs. M. Phillips; Mrs. L. Poston; The Public Record Office; Brion Purdey (Principal Librarian, Hastings Area); W. F. Scales (Chairman, Marlipins Museum, Shoreham); Mr. and Mrs. Fred Seymour; Mrs. Joyce Sleight (Archivist to Steyning Grammar School); Mr. Dave and Mrs. Rosie Stevens (Joint Secretaries of Steyning Athletic Club); Sussex Police, the Chief Constable; Peter Thorogood; James Wood; Mr. and Mrs. J. Wood; Mr. and Mrs. Lewis Wood; the late Harold Woolgar; John Woolgar; *Worthing and District Advertiser*, the Editor; Worthing Library, the Chief Librarian; Mrs. Sheila Wright.

To all the above I am most deeply indebted for the loan of their valuable photographs, their wide knowledge which they so willingly shared with me and their general help and support at all times. I must also thank my two local photographers who have spent so much time and effort on my behalf: K. Chalmers-Dixon and Jack Watkinson.

I am grateful to the following for permission to reproduce illustrations: Beeding and Bramber Local History Society, Bexhill Museum, Brighton Reference Library, British Library, Rev. B. Coote, Ian Dean (Director of Amberley Chalk Pits Museum), Mrs. Diana Durden, Mrs. Ruby Edmonds, Mrs. Gillian Fox, J. G. Garratt, J. S. Gray, John Green, Mrs. Joan Ham, Hastings Reference Library, Mr. and Mrs. A. Isaacs, Lens of Sutton, National Library of Ireland, Mr. Nethercoate-Bryant, Mrs. Phillips, F. Seymour, Mrs. Joyce Sleight, Steyning Athletic Club, Sussex Police Headquarters (Lewes), P. Thorogood, West Sussex Record Office, Mr. and Mrs. J. Wood, James Wood, Mr. and Mrs. Lewis Wood, Mr. John Woolgar, Worthing Reference Library.

The Rape of Bramber

Following his victory at the Battle of Hastings in 1066, William the Conqueror divided Sussex into rapes; these rapes were based on the original five Saxon burhs. Bramber rape was granted to William of Braose by 1073 and was known in the late 11th century by the name of its lord, or alternatively as the castelry of Steyning after its chief town.

Bramber rape stretches from the Surrey border in the north to the south coast; it takes in much of the range of chalk hills known as the South Downs. The coastal plain has always been fertile while the northern section is well wooded. Both the central and southern parts are drained by the River Adur and its tributaries. Originally the river formed a wide estuary but much of this land was later reclaimed. Evidence exists to suggest that both prehistoric man and later the Romans inhabited the southern portion of Bramber rape. During the Saxon period likewise this area was much favoured.

Edward the Confessor had given Steyning to the abbot of the great Benedictine monastery at Fécamp and it was still under his jurisdiction at the time of the Domesday Survey in 1086. Beeding too had belonged to the king but at Domesday it belonged jointly to William de Braose and William de Warenne of the rape of Lewes. Bramber itself was a late 11th-century 'new town'. Other settlements along the banks of the Adur estuary were at Coombes, Botolph's and Annington, though by the 14th century these last two had come to be considered as one vill. Since 1526 the former parish of Botolph's has been united for ecclesiastical purposes with Bramber parish. Today Coombes and Botolph's are little more than farmsteads – they may have been decimated at the time of the Black Death. Bramber and Beeding (sometimes called Upper Beeding in order to distinguish it from Lower Beeding some fifteen miles distant) are linked by a causeway road and virtually considered as one, though retaining their own identity and names.

Steyning

No evidence exists to suggest that Steyning was a settlement before the Saxon era; however, it is known that early man travelled the ancient trackways and during the Bronze age had a site on Round Hill, above Steyning. Later during the Romano-British period they built their temple on Chanctonbury, almost certainly on the site of a pre-existing Celtic one.

The north, west and south boundaries of Steyning follow these ancient ways while the site on the east-west crossroads may well have been the Saxon *Portus Cuthmanni*, for a major port certainly existed on the River Adur from Saxon times, if not earlier. The site of this early settlement was near the church, and Saxon remains have been found in this area. The river level was much higher than it is today and the port is thought to have been sited on an inlet, which has since disappeared. However, during severe flooding of the Adur in the winter of 1924-5 a wide creek formed in this locality, despite the silting of the river in the medieval period and the later embankment in the 19th century.

The town has been known by a variety of names, including Staninges in Domesday Book, the origins of which are obscure. It is thought to have some link with 'dwellers by a stony place', or alternatively it may refer to a prominent stone, or outcrop of sandstone found locally. The suffix 'ing' would suggest that the name is of Saxon origin, perhaps linked with a personal or family name.

The town, at the base of the South Downs on their north face, is set between two streams with the River Adur (previously a wide tidal estuary) running through the valley; thus it was well placed for water, both as a necessity of life, and as a means of transportation. Early in its history the focus of the town was nearer the church, and its development may have been planned on a rectangular grid with the main thoroughfare being Church Street. By the 18th century the area around the church had become somewhat isolated from the rest of the town.

Steyning is first mentioned in the legend of St Cuthman who founded a church there during the late eighth or ninth century. The playwright Christopher Fry based his story *The Boy With a Cart* on the saint's early life and his coming to Steyning. The 12th-century Norman church of St Andrew is thought to have been erected on the site of a previous Saxon church, built of wood, all trace of which has since disappeared. It is known to have housed a shrine to St Cuthman, which subsequently became a place of pilgrimage.

As early as A.D. 858 Steyning was under the patronage of the royal house of Wessex and because of its prime importance, King Ethelwulf (father of King Alfred) was first buried there in that year; later his remains were transferred to Winchester. Steyning continued to be royal land until about 1047 when much of it was granted by Edward the Confessor to the Norman Abbey of Fécamp. Subsequently the town was repossessed by Earl Godwin, father of King Harold, but after his defeat at the Battle of Hastings in 1066 it again reverted to Fécamp.

It is thought that the church was granted to Fécamp Abbey at the same time as Steyning but it retained its status as a royal free chapel. This was confirmed by King Edward I in 1290. Due to its special status Steyning church was exempt from any ecclesiastical jurisdiction except that of the Pope. The Abbey of Fécamp administered the town and established a college of secular canons there. The collegiate church was built under the supervision of the monks of Fécamp and it closely resembled the Romanesque churches of northern France.

During the reign of King Canute, Steyning had a mint with four moneyers attached, suggesting it was a town of some importance. This mint continued to operate until the reign of William II. Coins minted in the town have been found in this area of Sussex.

According to the Domesday Survey, Steyning was wasted following the Norman invasion and its value declined from £28 to £20, but within 20 years it had risen again to £25. The description of Steyning in Domesday Book shows it as a town of 123 burgages or dwellings, making it one of the larger towns in the south of England with a population estimated at around 1,500 inhabitants.

> Steyning continued to flourish as a market centre for the surrounding agricultural area with a Grant in 1272 to hold two fairs a year and a market twice a week. The port too was busy with a dockyard and a ship building industry. (*Steyning Conservation Area Guide*)

Steyning exported wood, wool and salt, the last commodity obtained from pans locally. Later the town lost its position of prestige to New Shoreham. According to Dr. T. P. Hudson:

> ... Steyning did not find its urban character until relatively late in its history; it was not included in the 'Burghal Hidage' and no definite provision was made in that document for the defence of the vulnerable Adur estuary.

The 'Burghal Hidage', a 10th-century taxation list, refers to burghs, specially constructed fortified settlements, which were erected in Sussex to combat the Danish raiders during the later Saxon period. These were at Hastings, Lewes, Burpham, Chichester and a fifth place called 'Heorepenburan' so far unidentified, but which may have been Pevensey.

During the 13th century severe storms swept Sussex, altering the coastline, changing the course of some rivers, and leading to the silting up of others, including the Adur. Whilst this silting was one of the contributory causes of the decline of the port of Steyning it was not necessarily the only one. By 1086 William de Braose (who had been granted Bramber rape by William the Conqueror) was charging tolls on traffic going to Steyning at his 'bridge' at Bramber and it has been suggested that another bridge built during the next century further impeded shipping bound for Steyning. The building by the de Braose family of the port of New Shoreham finally spelt doom for Steyning. Despite this, the town was of sufficient importance to return two members to Parliament in 1278, the year borough representation was established.

The port of Steyning had ceased to exist by 1350 and this, combined with a fall in population due to decimation by the Black Death in 1348, led to a period of stagnation. Within 100 years the town may well have regained some of its former prosperity, as many of the buildings standing today can be dated back to the 14th and 15th centuries.

At the time of the suppression of the alien priories, Steyning was repossessed by the Crown and passed into the hands of the Abbey of Sion, until the dissolution of the monasteries in 1534, when 'it reverted to the Crown and became part of the honor [sic] of Petworth'. Subsequently it passed into the possession of Thomas Howard, Duke of Norfolk, and remained under the control of the Norfolks until 1869, then to the Goring family before finally passing into individual ownership. The town was important enough to warrant holding Quarter Sessions there between the years 1667 and 1743 and adjourned sessions were held 10 times between 1774 and 1860. From the Norman period merchants and traders operated in Steyning, in particular those dealing in wine and cloth. However, only one Guild has been recorded, that of the Shoemakers and Tanners – this particular trade flourished until well into the present century. Mills and water-mills were built, one as early as about 1200 'when it was leased with the proviso that the wheat of the abbey's bailiff should be ground there toll-free'. The area surrounding the town was extensively cultivated and Steyning became one of the largest market towns in the south, and 'the skills of the ship-building industry were probably redeployed in the building industry ...' (*Steyning Guide*). With the growing numbers of successful merchants, fine houses (still in existence) were built both for and by them.

The medieval market must have been extremely diverse as Steyning lay only six miles from the port of New Shoreham. Many goods were brought into the town from Normandy and other continental countries, while goods produced locally would be collected and distributed from the town. As early as 1288 a market-place had been mentioned, the site of which has never been clearly ascertained. Later markets were held in the main streets, particularly High Street, Church Street and Sheep Pen Lane. The cattle fair was held on the first day of the Michaelmas Fair, usually 11 October. The second day was reserved for the Pleasure Fair. Some of the older residents of Steyning remember when:

> ... prior to the Fair every available meadow held its complement of lowing cattle. Many of the bullocks had been walked by road from as far away as Wales, some of them having been shod with kews for the journey. On Fair Day these cattle were sold in the George Meadow opposite Penn's House, and in the Mill Field near Charlton Court Mill. Welsh cattle were usually sold in the George Meadow and other breeds in the Mill Field. All sales were by private treaty and no auction took place. (*Memories of Steyning* by C. Grigg.)

With the coming of the railway in 1861 an auction market began nearer the station and the one in the town centre ceased. Annual horse sales commenced during the 1890s and continued to be held until well into this century, when they were among the largest in southern England.

Trade declined when a 'new' market at Broadwater was held on the same day as Steyning, but by the early 18th century the town once again became a market centre of regional importance. 'In 1730 there was a market every Friday and on the second Wednesday of each month. Besides the two old fairs there was another held on 29 May.'

At the turn of the 19th century Steyning became an alternative meeting place with Horsham for shows of the Bramber Agricultural Society and the meeting-place for regular prize shows of fat stock. According to the *Steyning Conservation Area Guide*, 'the market and fairs kept the town alive, but there was little expansion'.

From early in its history Steyning had its own brewery, and at one time, two. Beer was distributed locally to beer retailers and tied-inns within the town. It is thought that the hops were in the main grown elsewhere. By the 19th century both breweries had their own malthouses. Allied trades flourished, such as coopers who made the barrels in which the beer was stored. The building trade was one of the earliest in the town. Lime-pits were recorded in 1568 and brick works in the next century.

The town was the centre of a rich agricultural region, sheep farming being highly profitable, and later arable. By the 19th century dairy farming became popular, especially after the opening of the railway – the coastal resorts took most of the dairy produce. Steyning had its own forges and wheelwrights and by 1862 the manufacture of farm machinery was recorded. *Kelly's Directory* for 1895 records a Veterinary Surgeon practising in the town. Other trades flourished in order to serve the rising number of inhabitants.

By the mid-19th century two main trades employed much of the local labour – the breweries and the skin and hide processors. The opening of the tanyard in the 1830s led to a growth in related trades, such as fellmongers, woolstaplers, tanners, parchment makers, harness and saddle makers and shoe makers. In order to facilitate trade, a bank had opened in 1798 with others following in the 19th century. However, this growth in industry was not to last and, according to Hudson, 'During the 20th century an increasingly large proportion of the parish have worked outside it ...'.

Throughout its history the River Adur has played an important part in the development of the town. It was originally used for the transportation of goods, but as early as the 14th century meat and cider were transported from Steyning to Shoreham by road. The implementation of the River Adur Navigation Act in the reign of George III led to an increase in water-borne traffic, so that even as late as 1938 barges were in use on the river.

Unlike the nearby coastal towns with their long military tradition, Steyning was not considered of sufficient importance to warrant garrisons being stationed there, except during times of great national crisis. In 1586 and 1626 the town became a store for military supplies. Again, during the Napoleonic wars, barracks were built for use by an infantry division. These were demolished at the end of hostilities and the only remaining link with the past is a house in Jarvis Lane which at one time served as the officers' quarters. Nonetheless the inhabitants of Steyning were never ill prepared to face an enemy, for as early as the 15th century bowmen practised archery in 'The Shooting Field', which from 1519 belonged to Steyning parish church.

In 1555 one of the Marian martyrdoms took place in Steyning. The place of execution may have been Chantry Green. The Protestant, John Launder, was burnt at the stake for refusing to renounce his religious beliefs during the reign of 'Bloody' Queen Mary. Despite the feeling of revulsion that must have followed his death, no undue pressure appears to have been brought to bear on those practising the Roman Catholic faith in and around Steyning, though by 1767 there were only two recusants remaining in the town. The Roman Catholics returned to Steyning in the middle of this century and were given the town hall to use as a centre for the celebration of mass. However, by 1951 a barn at Penlands Farm was converted as the Church of Christ the King.

Steyning has not at any time been remarkable for that radical Nonconformity which has influenced life in the more industrial north. George Fox, one of the founders of the Quaker movement, was permitted to preach at a meeting held in the Market House in 1655 and later Quakers had a meeting house in the town known as Penn's House, in honour of the well-known Quaker and founder of Pennsylvania, U.S.A., who preached there during the 17th century. The Quakers were also allowed to bury their dead in the ground adjoining it. There was a chapel for Wesleyan Methodists in Steyning in 1835, despite the fact that for much of that century it was without a resident minister. Likewise, the Baptists had a place of worship in the High Street around 1804 but due to a fall in their numbers the chapel closed. Even the Salvation Army appeared to meet with religious tolerance within the town.

Certain writers described Steyning in the past as 'much decayed', but this is thought to have been an exaggeration, though it is recognised that there was a decline in population between the 16th and 18th centuries. Apparently only thirty parishioners had the county franchise in 1705. Nevertheless Steyning continued to return two Members of Parliament but by the 19th century it had become one of the 'Decayed and Rotten Boroughs', with a reputation for vote rigging. Under the Reform Act of 1832, Steyning lost its right to Parliamentary representation.

From earliest times Steyning, because of its strategic position, has been a centre of communications for the east-west traffic through the county and by the 18th century the Horsham-Steyning road had become an alternative route from London to Brighton. Coaches ran between the town and London and only ceased operating with the opening of the railway in 1861. Within living memory a coach and four used to run from Brighton to the *White Horse Hotel* in Steyning during the summer months. Previously this hotel had served as a posting house for the changing of horses *en route* between London and Worthing. The fare for this journey was apparently one shilling for outside passengers and two shillings and sixpence for those travelling inside the coach in 1803 (Grigg). The coming of the railway ended the coaching era but brought revival to Steyning.

Innkeepers had been recorded in Steyning from the 15th century. Two of the earliest inns, the *White Horse* and the *Chequer*, have survived until today, though much of the former was destroyed by a disastrous fire in 1949. It is thought that the sign of the chequer denotes that it was used for business transactions when the markets were held in the High Street, the chequer-board being an aid to counting. Both these inns served other purposes throughout their long existence. The *White Horse* was used intermittently as a town hall and borough court, while the *Chequer* accommodated public meetings, including the hundred court. Other inns and beer-houses flourished in the town and, according to *Kelly's Directory* for 1890, at least 12 inhabitants of Steyning were involved in the sale of beer and other alcoholic beverages.

The Old Market House in the High Street originally served as the town hall but in 1886 a purpose-built structure was erected, which today is used as a permanent court-house. During the 19th century the town's two wells, Singwell and Britain's well, had pumps attached to them and the main streets were paved; gas lighting had appeared by mid-century to be followed by electric lighting early in the 20th century. The town had its own fire-engine which for a time was housed in the Old Market House. As early as 1675 a thrice-weekly postal service was begun, while just over 200 years later letters were despatched from the town five times during weekdays and once on Sundays. Carriers operated to Brighton and Shoreham three times a week, returning the same day, while according to *Kelly's Directory* for 1895 the L.B. & S.C. Railway Company employed their own carrier within the town.

Domesday Book shows Steyning as having two churches, one dedicated to St Cuthman, the other to St Mary. No definite evidence exists as to the whereabouts of the latter. Anna M. Butler, writing *The History of Steyning and its Church* which was published in 1913, suggested that it was situated on the south side of the High Street, while other historians feel a site at Bidlington more likely in view of the fact that there was probably a hospital for lepers there, with a church or chapel dedicated in honour of St Mary Magdalen around the 13th century.

The church dedicated to St Andrew, being collegiate, was regarded as a 'Royal Free Chapel', with its own provost or dean. It possessed two sanctuary knockers on both the inner and outer doors, and two murderers are believed to have sought sanctuary there in 1280. Throughout its history the church appears to have suffered badly from neglect. The Nonae Return of 1341 showed that it belonged to Fécamp, with the Abbot as 'lord and rector'. Two hundred years later it was stated to be very much ruined and decayed. The original plan may have been a cruciform aisled church, with central tower, but as the church stands today the work ends at the crossing. The present tower was built by public subscription and replaces two earlier ones.

It is safe to assume that Steyning with its collegiate church certainly had a school long before the 16th century. Five schoolmasters were mentioned in the parish between 1579 and 1607 and 'the first master of the grammar school after its endowment in 1614 had been licensed to teach in Steyning in 1609' (Grigg). During the 19th century there were four elementary schools, and Steyning National school founded in 1812, together with a number of private ones, many of them short-lived boarding schools. Steyning County Secondary Modern School opened in 1953 and in 1968 it amalgamated with the grammar school as a co-educational comprehensive school called Steyning Grammar School, with over 2,000 pupils on its roll coming both from the town and a wide catchment area.

The playing of tennis had been recorded in Steyning as early as 1481 but the subsequent years saw little in the way of cultural activities, until well into the 19th century. A Mechanics' Institute was recorded in 1855. According to Lowerson and Myerscough, 'the original concept was for the poorer classes to set up improving, mutuality clubs of their own, although usually under suitable guidance'. This century saw the introduction of entertainments on a lighter note with the formation of an operatic society, a horticultural society and cricket and football clubs. One activity, the Annual Easter Monday Walking Race, has become internationally famous.

Steyning became popular this century with writers. William Butler Yeats, who won the Nobel Prize for Literature in 1923, frequently stayed in the town. Victor B. Neuberg, while a resident there, produced his own poems on a hand-operated printing press. Naturally many artists have also been attracted to such a delightful locality, including James Whistler, the famous Anglo-American painter.

With the advent of the railway, Steyning expanded to the north-west. The greatest development took place this century, particularly after the end of World War II, with the population increasing rapidly. Today the town has changed from a place of pilgrimage to a haunt for the rising number of tourists both from home and abroad, though much of Steyning still has the air of a prosperous medieval town.

Much of the information contained in this introduction has been taken from an article in *Sussex History*, 'The Origins of Steyning and Bramber', by T. P. Hudson and from Dr. Hudson's article in *Victoria County History* vol. 6 part 1 (1980). All quotations are taken from this unless otherwise stated. For readers wishing to verify the original sources I would suggest reference be made to this volume.

Churches

1. St Andrew's church, Steyning from a 19th-century drawing by R. H. Nibbs. At one time this 12th-century church was much larger, possibly cruciform in design. The chancel of the Norman church extended east of the present churchyard and, as the ground falls away sharply, was evidently carried on an undercroft, which is thought to have incorporated the shrine of St Cuthman. After the dissolution of the monasteries the eastern parts of the church fell into decay and by the early 17th century the chancel and part of the nave were demolished. In 1750 or thereabouts the chancel was rebuilt in Gothic style. Further restoration work took place during the 19th century.

2. Steyning church and vicarage from the north-east in 1781, from a pen-and-wash drawing by S. H. Grimm. Today the vicarage is known as The Old Priory as its site is presumably identical to that of the medieval college. In this picture it is shown as a half-timbered house, but some years later it was considerably altered.

3. This drawing by Grimm, dated 1780, shows the splendid clerestoried nave of the church of St Andrew, with its magnificent columns and decorated arches.

4. In 1865 Rev. Thomas Medland, Vicar of Steyning, presented this lychgate to the parish. In the churchyard behind are the remains of James Day of the North Hants. Light Infantry, who is reputed to have been flogged to death for a minor offence. The stone marking his grave was apparently erected by his comrades. This photograph was taken *c*.1904.

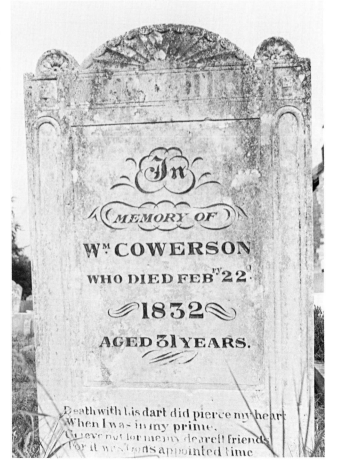

5. Among the interesting tombstones in St Andrew's churchyard is one to William Cowerson, a smuggler killed by excisemen in 1832. Cowerson, a bricklayer by trade, was a local man and, judging from the length of his grave, a very tall one. According to local records, Cowerson was the leader of a gang of smugglers and in a fight near Broadwater broke the arm of one excise officer with his cudgel before being shot dead by another. His body was returned to Steyning on a waggon. At his funeral, it is said that 'the church bells rang a merry peal'.

6. The tithe barn which once stood close to the church of St Andrew. Today the vicarage stands on this site.

7. This photograph shows the wonderful detail of the Norman carving on the arches and the capitals of the massive columns within the church of St Andrew. Today the upper gallery has been removed and one can appreciate the beauty of this church.

8. A photostat copy of the Charter (which hangs in the church) signed by William the Conqueror, his son William Rufus, Archbishop Lanfranc and four others. This Charter confirmed King Edward the Confessor's gift of 'St Cuthman's Church' to the Holy Church at Fécamp. The original Charter is in the possession of the Abbey of Fécamp, but unfortunately all other documents relating to this gift were destroyed during the French Revolution of 1789.

9. Stone gargoyle on the church. Legend has it that this depicts the only silent woman in Steyning!

10. Seventeenth-century carved panels depicting the life of St Cuthman, originally over the mantelpiece in the house of Colonel Broad at Branscombe, Dorset. St Cuthman has long been associated with the town of Steyning. He was not Sussex born but is reputed to have come to the area as a young man, conveying his aged mother in a type of wheelbarrow which he propelled with the aid of a rope around his shoulders. When the rope broke he used elder twigs. Peasants haymaking in a field nearby laughed at his efforts, whereupon a storm broke out, ruining their hay. Cuthman resolved to build a church on the spot where the elder twigs themselves gave way. The Saxon church at Steyning was certainly known as St Cuthman's and the port as Portus Cuthmanni.

11. George Fox visited Steyning in 1655 and was allowed by the constable to hold a meeting in the Market Hall, which led to the establishment of a Quaker community there. By 1678 the Quakers had acquired their own meeting-house with a common burial ground; the men were buried on one side and women on the other. William Penn, who founded the state of Pennsylvania, U.S.A., preached at this house which came to be known as 'Penn's House' and remained in Quaker hands for two centuries. During the present century meetings were held in another building until 1967 when the Quakers again acquired and met in the meeting-house.

Streets and Buildings

12. Today the whole length of the main road of Steyning is known as the High Street, but over a hundred years ago the name applied only to the part from Church Street to the Horsham Road. The lower part, from Jarvis Lane to Lintott's Corner, was for centuries known as Singwell Street. On the left of this picture, taken around 1900, a pump can be seen attached to the well which throughout the centuries has supplied Steyning with a constant water supply.

13. The village pump early this century – this still stands at the southern end of the High Street. Nearby was a well covered by a shingled roof and known as the Shingled Well. This name was later corrupted to Singwell. As will be noted there are actually two pumps at different levels. There was a further pump at the opposite end of the town.

14. Steyning High Street pre-1914. In the distance on the right can be seen Market House with its distinctive clock. The vicar, Rev. Congreve-Pridgeon, is talking to Colonel Young. The cattle appear to be roaming free and it seems ironical that they have stopped opposite a butcher's shop!

15. Outside the *Chequer Inn*, c.1920. This ancient building, once an important coaching inn on the London-south coast routes, is said to date from the 15th century, but during the 19th century a new façade covered the original half-timbered one. At the time the Hundred Court was held here. The Chequer sign was apparently an indication to traders that a checkered cloth or board was kept at the inn in order to help them to settle their accounts from the weekly market which took place in the street outside. In the distance can be seen the *White Horse Hotel*, the other posting stop in Steyning. This inn was completely destroyed by fire in 1949 – the present building has been converted from the old stables and outbuildings.

16. High Street looking south-west, at the junction of Church Street and Sheep Pen Lane. Due to the snowy conditions underfoot three different types of handcart seem to be in use, and the delivery boy on the corner is carrying a large basket as used by bakers and butchers as late as the 1950s.

17. Carved beam in the present post office in Steyning High Street.

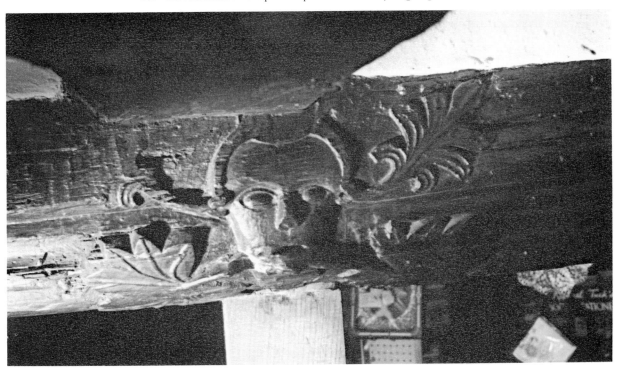

18. An artist's impression of Church Street, c.1800.

19. Church Street, c.1860. This is believed to be one of the earliest photographs of Steyning. Church Street has always been an important thoroughfare in the town, with Brotherhood Hall, a forge, a cooper's and a public house all within a few yards of one another. The covered handcart on the left may have been used for the delivery of bread.

CHURCH ST STEYNING ABOUT 1860.

20. Church Street in the days of horse-drawn traffic, c.1900. On the right is Saxon Cottage with its unique 'cat's slide roof', said to have been constructed without the use of nails. Despite its name, this house is a 16th-century building. Today few children would risk standing in the middle of the road to be photographed.

21.   In 1729 the parish vestry decided to purchase a building to house the local poor and allocated the sum of £100. This 15th-century timber-framed building thus became the workhouse for the paupers. In 1734 certain of the poor from neighbouring Beeding were included, the authorities paying £5 per annum for their admission. By 1758 the Master of the workhouse was paid the princely sum of £140 to cover all expenses incurred.

Women teachers were paid 2s. per week to instruct the young inmates, those under nine years of age. From then until reaching the age of 21, they were put out to work as parish apprentices. On 11 September 1835 a serious riot took place in Steyning, due to the wider Union of Parishes and the consequent breaking-up of families within the workhouse. The fighting lasted a scant four hours, with the townspeople supporting the authorities. Ten men and two women were sent for trial at Lewes Assizes the following March. The workhouse was closed later in 1835. This photograph shows the building when it was divided into two cottages, c.1900.

22.   The Stone House (right), on the corner of Sheep Pen Lane, is said to be the oldest building in Steyning apart from the church. It has been used for many purposes, including a 'Clothehalle' and subsequently a gaol. Local tradition claims that it may stand on the site of a Saxon Mint. The heavily laden waggon in this photograph is en route to the railway station with a load of bales. The tannery in Tanyard Lane was owned by G. T. Breach & Sons and a number of Steyning men and boys were involved in the allied trades, such as fellmongers, woolstaplers, tanners and parchment makers. The tanyard was a central point for the collection and sorting of sheep-skins and hides. The former were processed locally by the men employed at the 'yard'. While the stench from a tannery is somewhat obnoxious, it is nevertheless a very healthy occupation and was at one time recommended for those suffering from tuberculosis!

23.   Coin minted in Steyning during the reign of King William I. The Stone House may have been the site of the Steyning Mint, but this cannot be verified. Silver pennies struck in the town during the Saxon era have been found, bearing the effigies of Edward the Confessor and Harold. In 1866 a hoard of silver pennies and other coins were ploughed up in a field at Lower Chancton Farm, Wiston, 11 of them having been minted in Steyning.

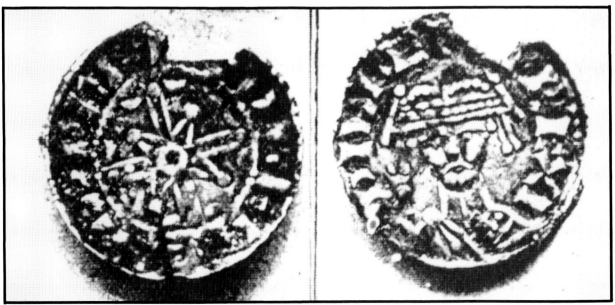

24. A very old cottage in Church Side. The man standing in the doorway drove the Worthing to London coach for years. The building gradually became more and more dilapidated and by 1904 it had been demolished.

25. Shoes found hidden in the eaves of a local house. They were probably placed heel upward on the top of the house of relatively poor occupants in order to protect it.

Steyning People

26.   Early education was normally in the hands of the Church. It is safe to assume that Steyning, with its collegiate church of St Andrew, had a school long before the 16th century; however, Leonard Mitchell (1584) is the earliest recorded licensed school-master. The Grammar School was endowed by William Holland, a Steyning man, in 1614. This picture shows a school group, *c*.1883. The headmaster at that time was Rev. Alfred Harre, who retired in 1908. The previous headmaster had been George Airey, who had been particularly successful in building up the reputation of the school. However, after 37 years of his headship, the material fabric of the school was in a terrible state and the school was closed for six years while the buildings were renovated and modernised. Following this work the living accommodation was increased to take up to 25 boarders (about half the total of pupils), and fees were £8 p.a.

27. Mr. and Mrs. George Burgess Michell in about 1895. Mr. Michell owned the brewery adjacent to their home, 'Charlton House'. It had a good water supply but suffered from its cramped surroundings and the fact that its malt house was in Church Street. Mr. Michell also owned certain farms in the Lancing area. During the present century the brewery ceased operating and merged with the Rock and Portsmouth Breweries.

28. Kenneth, Eric and young Noel, sons of George Burgess Michell, *c.*1890. None of the boys elected to follow their father into the brewery business.

29. & 30. Charles Stewart Parnell, one of the greatest Irish leaders of all time who led Ireland to the brink of Home Rule, married Katherine O'Shea at Steyning Registrar's Office, No.2 Gordon House, on 25 June 1891. Parnell was considered by his contemporaries to be among the most handsome of men in the House of Commons while Katherine was described as rather plump, with heavy features, but a vivacious personality. Their adulterous relationship commenced in 1880 and it is believed that Katherine's husband, Captain O'Shea, was a party to this. In 1886 the first allusion to the love affair appeared in the *Irish Times* and by 1890 the Captain and his wife were divorced and he resigned from Parliament.
Mrs. O'Shea was the mother of six children, two daughters by Parnell, Clare born in 1883 and Frances a year later. On the marriage certificate there seems to be a discrepancy over Katherine's age. She is recorded as 40 and Parnell as 44, even though she was born in 1846, the same year as Parnell. Parnell himself only lived for a few months after his wedding, which finally caused his political downfall.

31. Charles Goring was responsible for planting the circle of beech trees at Chanctonbury Ring on the crest of the South Downs in 1760. It is said that he carried buckets of water to the seedlings from his home at Wiston below the site of this early hill-fort. The ring of trees was visible for more than 30 miles across the countryside and dominates the Downs behind Steyning and the valley of the river Adur. During World War Two there was talk of cutting down this famous ring of trees as they were an obvious landmark for enemy planes. Sadly this view is very different today, following the destruction by the hurricane on the night of 16 October 1987.

32. Wiston House, the home of the Goring family, once very important landowners in the county. The Dukes of Norfolk inherited many of the houses and certain lands in the hundred of Steyning, as shown in the Steyning Tithe Award of 1835, while the Gorings owned property in the Arundel area. During the last century many of these properties were interchanged. Wiston House was erected in the 16th century and modernised in 1844. Admiral Sir Charles Matthews Goring acquired the estate in 1743.

33. A group of children in Elm Grove early this century.

34. Albert Coote, aged 99, riding his bicycle around Steyning. Today this centenarian is still enjoying life in the town where he came to work as a young man of 16. He became a market gardener and continued this work for 25 years. In World War One he served in the Royal Army Medical Corps, while during World War Two he was an auxiliary fireman.

Agriculture

35.   Early Steyning is thought to have been in the area close to the church, Gatewick mill and Gatewick house. The mill, one of two in Steyning, ceased operating in 1878 and was demolished. The house is named after the de Gatewick family which had early connections with the town. This lithograph of the house in about 1860 shows it as a farm before restoration work.

36. Early in its history Steyning had four water mills; two continued to operate well into the 19th century and on the same stream. Court Mill was worked until 1927, when it belonged to the Steyne Food Company, suppliers of cattle and poultry food. Today it has been converted into private accommodation. The above picture shows the mill pond *c*.1906.

37. The mill-wheel at Court Mill, made by a local wheelwright, Mr. C. A. Woolgar, in his wheelwright's shop in School Lane. At the time this drawing was made (1926) the mill was still operating.

38. The cattle market in Church Street, 1890, from a painting by F. Jennings. In the distance can be seen the Old Grammar School, with its square central tower, before it was raised in the last century. Note the barrels outside the cooper's premises. With two breweries and a malt house in Steyning, they were kept very busy.

39. One of the best-known pictures of Steyning showing the cattle market, c.1890, when it was held in the High Street. On the left is the façade of the *White Horse*. Sheep were often confined to pens in Newham Lane, originally called le Schepenestrete in 1271, while bullocks were tied to the railings in Church Street. Later the market was moved to the station site, making it easier to transport stock via the railway. The two men front centre are Messrs. Cheriman, a butcher, and his assistant, Tasker. On the right is Lasmar Penfold, a well-known Steyning character. Mr. Joyes from the *White Horse Inn* and another butcher, Mr. Heryett, can also be identified.

40. Steyning cattle market was started *c*.1890 on land which had been originally part of Steyning Glebe, but was later purchased by the LB & SC Railway. An earlier market had been held in the town centre, but conditions there were too cramped. This photograph is of the Fat Stock Show of 1930 with Mr. Leslie Burt the auctioneer.

41. Steyning Young Farmers' Club, *c*.1932, with calves. It is interesting to note that many of the youngsters are wearing school uniform, complete with regulation velour hats.

42. An annual horse sale was held at Steyning from about 1890 until well into this century. It was reputed to be one of the largest of its kind in the south of England. In this 1937 photograph, the auctioneer can be seen standing in the waggon.

43. Steyning Fat Stock show: South Down wether lambs, Class 9, *c.*1930.

GIFT SALE

in aid of the

Royal Agricultural Benevolent Institution

**(Under the auspices of the National Farmers' Union,
Steyning Branch)**

to be held in the

Steyning Cattle Market

on

WEDNESDAY, 25th MAY, 1932

(By kind permission of Mr. W. LESLIE BURT, Hon. Auctioneer).

LIVE STOCK GIFTS, Sheep, Pigs, Etc., will be sold in their
class during the ordinary Market.

SALE of ALL OTHER GIFTS will take place in the MARKET
FIELD commencing at 3.45 p.m.

REFRESHMENTS from 12 noon by the Ladies' Catering
Department.

SPECIAL SALE STALL by the Ladies.

SPECIAL SALE of STRONG DURABLE BASKETS made
by the West of England Institution for
the Blind.

WEIGHT JUDGING COMPETITIONS, SIDE SHOWS, ETC.

Fullest Support of this very deserving cause is solicited.

" Many can help one while one cannot help many."

44. Poster advertising a Gift Sale in aid of the Royal Agricultural Benevolent Institution.
Steyning was a very important centre for agriculture with an active market, but in the 1930s
farming was suffering from a severe depression which caused much hardship to both the
farming community and the labouring classes.

45.   Loading potatoes on Cross's Farm, Steyning, *c*.1932. The rolling Downs were once covered in sheep.

46.   Sheep yards or standing folds on the South Downs. Today the art of constructing these wattle hurdles is almost dead. Arthur Young in his *General View of the Agriculture of the County of Sussex* (1813) stated that 'between East Bourne [sic] and Steyning which is 33 miles the Downs are about 6 miles wide and in this tract there are about 200,000 ewes kept, with numbers rising to 270,000 sheep in Summer, the rate of stocking not exceeded in any part of England'.

A SUSSEX SHEPHERD ON THE SOUTH DOWNS, STEYNING.
HIS BEST COMPANIONS INNOCENCE & HEALTH AND HIS BEST RICHES IGNORANCE OF WEALTH
GOLDSMITH

Earning a Living

47.   The Post Office pre-1920 before it was transferred to its present building, showing one of the postmen and a telegraph boy.

48.   Mr. F. Seymour's greengrocery in the High Street, *c*.1936. Mrs. Nellie Rason is in the centre of the window with Mr. Seymour in the doorway.

49. Mr. Lewis Wood as a toddler with his parents, *c.*1910. His father, Mr. C. F. Wood, started his Motor Engineering Works in the High Street, and his son expanded this into a garage. Mr. Lewis Wood ran the first taxi service in the town. Note the boots and shoes hanging up outside the draper's, probably produced at the local tannery.

50. These three cars, delivered in Steyning on the same day in March 1925, were all ordered by local residents. Mr. Wood senior is standing outside the showroom, while his young son Lewis Wood is seated in the driving seat of the Singer car. It was he who later used to travel to the Works at Coventry and Birmingham in order to drive the vehicles back to Steyning, a round journey that took over 14 hours to complete: the charge for this service was £2.50 per car. Today the cost would be £1,000 for eight or ten cars delivered by transporter.

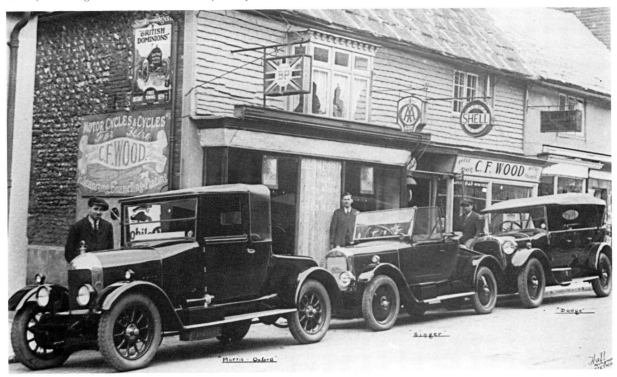

51.   The International Stores were the first of the multiple stores to arrive in Steyning. This photograph was taken *c*.1910.

52.   Steyning's fine police station was built about 1856. This photograph shows officers of the Steyning division of the West Sussex Constabulary outside the police station some time before World War One. None of the officers are wearing ribbons of that time, but one officer is wearing the Queen's South Africa medal indicating service in the Boer War. The West Sussex Constabulary was formed in 1857 with its headquarters and House of Correction at Petworth. The busy Steyning division had men at Southwick, Shoreham, Washington and Storrington, an area which they had to patrol on foot. In 1889 there were 16 men in the division.

53. This building has served a variety of purposes. Formerly the town hall, it has also been called Sessions House and Market House, suggesting that quarter sessions were held there and market tolls collected. The building is earlier than the clock turrret which was erected by public subscription in 1848-9 in order to house the clock, a gift to Steyning by the Duke of Norfolk. Earlier drawings of the High Street show the clock cantilevered over the road. By about 1900 the building was used as the fire station and the horse-drawn engine is visible in the doorway. The horses were normally kept at the *White Horse Inn* and, when the fire bell rang, they were untied and made their own way along the street to the fire station. Next door is the shop of T. Carr & Son, Bootmaker, one of a number in a town which had a thriving tannery.

AT
ABINGWORTH
FIRE,
JAN 17 1910

54. Steyning fire brigade in 1910 when it had a horse-drawn Merryweather engine. The men had been attending a fire near Storrington, which had no brigade of its own at that time.

55. P. Oliver, fire chief at Steyning, *c.*1906.

56. It has been impossible to ascertain whether this was a 'practice run' or an actual fire. Early in the 19th century Steyning had a town fire-engine, housed in the town hall. Later this service was taken over by the parish council.

57. Steyning's first motor fire engine outside the early fire station in the Old Market House in 1924/25.

Old Malthouse, Chantry Green Steyning, About 1898.

58.   The Old Malthouse, Chantry Green, sketched by G. de Paris and dated 1890. Barley or other grain was normally steeped in water until germination and then dried in a kiln before being brewed. With two breweries, Gates and Michells, later amalgamated and known as the Steyning Breweries, this malthouse must have been kept extremely busy. It was demolished in 1902. A second malthouse in Jarvis Lane belonged to Gates' Brewery; it was later used as an indoor miniature rifle range.

59.   The southern end of the High Street, c.1905. On the right is one of Steyning's pumps and the chimney of Gates' Brewery complex can be seen left of centre. On market days, calves were weighed in a scale from a hook in one of the trees behind the barrow. During the early years of this century the two breweries called their workers by means of a hooter. The men must have made quite a noise walking through the town in their pattens, part of their normal working attire.

60. At one time the present St Andrew's Hall was part of the Gates' Brewery complex, part of which was destroyed by a fire in 1917. This picture shows some of the plant.

61. A painting of Church Street, *c.*1860, with a horse in the doorway of the forge. There was another forge in the High Street, where kews (or ox shoes) were made.

62. Tweed Brothers' Forge in Church Street, *c.*1920. A blacksmith had worked in these premises as early as 1670.

63. The Tweed brothers, Fred and Horace, at work in their forge in Church Street.

64. Charles Woolgar outside the wheelwright works in School Lane. The Woolgars were a well-known family of wheelwrights who had forges and wheelwright businessses in Steyning, Bramber, Beeding and Storrington. A member of the Guild of Sussex Craftsmen, Charles Woolgar is shown here with wheels which he made for the Three Bridges Southern Agricultural Show in 1933.

65. Two types of cart among the 40 or so patterns for vehicles produced by the Woolgar family from about 1880 until just before World War Two. The pattern book is still in existence.

39

66. F. Duke, Ltd., builders, decorators and timber merchants, were one of the chief employers in Steyning for over 80 years, the firm having been founded in 1902. Frank Duke is the central figure standing with his hands in his pocket. The photograph was taken in about 1930.

67. Saw-pit in operation sometime before World War One, possibly on the Wiston Estate. The junior workman normally worked in the pit itself. Bark from the logs may have been sent to Steyning Tannery.

68. The first premises of J. Wood, Butcher, on the junction of Chantry Green and Church Street, *c.*1910. On 23 July 1555 Protestant John Launder was burnt at the stake on Chantry Green, during the reign of the Catholic Queen Mary.

69. Wood's family butchers in the High Street, *c.*1915, showing the horse and cart used for deliveries.

Transport

70. The *White Horse*, c.1900, before this frontage was destroyed by fire in 1949. The name of this inn derives from the arms of the dukes of Norfolk who had close connections with Steyning over the centuries. The inn has existed since 1614 and at various times has been used for borough courts, quarter sessions and public meetings. In 1855 the inn was a posting house and an excise and inland revenue office. Later it became an agency for the London and Brighton railway, running coaches to and from the station.

71. A facsimile of a poster advertising coaching to London. Both the *White Horse* and the *Chequer Inn* became important posting stops on the London to south coast run.

72. Steyning stationmaster and other employees of the railway some 60 years ago. Note the two boys included in the picture, the younger one wearing the round grey velour hat of the period and high laced boots with black stockings.

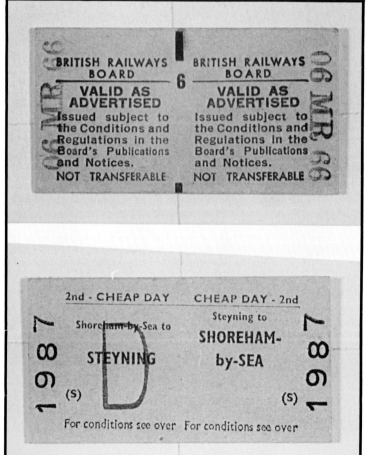

73. The railway from Shoreham to Horsham via Steyning lasted a scant hundred years. During the 19th century the railway restored Steyning as an important market centre – cattle pens were erected at the station and roads thereabouts were developed. Today only the warehouse remains of the railway complex and this, according to Pevsner, is 'still Georgian in its proportions'. The station was built by Mr. Chappell, *c.*1860. He was the contractor responsible for most of the buildings constructed on the Shoreham to Horsham section of the London, Brighton and South Coast Railway.

74. A ticket from the last day the trains ran between Steyning and Shoreham-by-Sea, 6 March 1966. Much of the Steyning by-pass follows the same route as the railway.

Leisure and Pleasure

75. Old people sitting on the seat in Steyning cricket ground on a peaceful Whit Monday, 1 June 1914. It is difficult to imagine that within a few months Europe would be plunged into the horrors of World War One.

76.   A tug-of-war in the recreation ground in 1910. The two boys taking part may have been pupils of the Grammar School.

77.   Fête in Steyning recreation ground in the early 1900s. The policeman was Bob Wareham and the clergyman may have been Rev. Arthur Congreve-Pridgeon B.A., who was vicar from 1882 to 1918.

Rapley.   Watson.   Coleman.   Parlett.   Chalcraft.   Lawrence.   Adcock.   Fuller.

Thompson.   Norden.   Oliver.   Green.   Mitchell.

78.   A postcard showing Steyning football club 1907-8 with the names of the players. This card was sent by Wallie Lawrence (third from right, standing) to his father in Canada. He stated that the picture was taken before a match with Horsham. Steyning lost the game by 2-1, but had apparently beaten Southwick the previous week.

HALL
STEYNING

Meet of the HORSHA[

79. The Crawley and
Horsham hunt at Steyning.
The early history of this hunt
is obscure. The first Master
was a Mr. Stanford, *c*.1847.
From 1847-67 the hounds
were kennelled at
Warninglid, afterwards
Staplefield, and then from
1877 at West Grinstead. The
hunt covers a very wide area,
from Ockley in Surrey to
Worthing, a distance of 25
miles from north to south
and 20 miles from east to
west, of mainly woodland or
agricultural land.

EBRA

1300
POULTR

CRAWLEY Foxhounds at STEYNING. No 2.

80. In 1903 the members of the Steyning 'Ping-Pong' Club, who had their headquarters in the *Norfolk Arms*, were arguing about the London-Brighton walk. They took bets as to who, at that time, was the club's fastest walker. A 15-mile road walking race, starting outside the public house in Church Street and returning to the town via the outlying villages, was suggested and on 6 May this took place with 15 men competing. The winner was Horace Green, seated on the ground on the far left. Apparently many of the competitors had done little or no training. They resorted to liquor as a stimulant and ultimately completed the course lying on a sack in the back of a coal merchant's van. Seven entrants completed the race and the winner's time was 2 hours 53 minutes.

Official Programme 2d.

Steyning and District

ANNUAL

WALKING RACES

ON

EASTER MONDAY

April 13th, 1925.

Open to persons residing in Steyning, Wiston, Ashurst, Bramber, Beeding, Small Dole and Cement Works.

OFFICIALS.

President :—Dr. C. W. WHEELER-BENNETT.
Chairman :—Mr. G. T. BREACH.
Starter :—Dr. C. W. WHEELER-BENNETT.
Judge :—Mr. W. WARE.
Timekeepers :—Messrs. W. J. SPRINKS & S. MATTHEWS.
Marshalls of the Course :—Messrs. E. HARMAN & R. STILGOE.
Collector :—Mr. H. LINDFIELD.
Hon. Treasurer :—Mr. R. BATEMAN.
Hon. Secretary :—Mr. D. WEST.
At the Tape :—Messrs. P. E. KILLPARTRICK & W. W. RAPLEY.

COURSE STEWARDS.

Messrs. A. COOPER, F. GANDER, A. GREEN, H. LINDFIELD,
A. T. MILLS, C. T. SEARLE, F. STUBBINGS, J. STONEHAM,
H. STAMMER, E. TELLICK and G. TIDEY.

SPECIAL NOTICE.—The Police particularly request that everyone *must* keep behind the ropes during the start and finish of each Race.

Bateman's Printing Works, Steyning, Sussex.

81. Official programme of the Steyning and District Annual Walking Races held on Easter Monday 13 April 1925. At this time the route was from Steyning town clock, through Partridge Green, Henfield, Bramber and back to the finishing line at the clock. Earlier in the century the races had started from Church Street. Until 1920 the races were contested on a handicap basis and offered prizes of tradesmen's vouchers. Throughout the 1930s the races were dominated by John Henderson, who set up a record time which was not broken for 24 years. Mr. Henderson was a founder member of Steyning Athletic Club, today recognised as one of the premier walking clubs in the country.

82. An early photograph of the walking race. Note the enthusiasm of the crowd, very noticeable on the faces of the children.

83. During the 1930s younger boys clamoured to take part in the Steyning walking races. Prior to this, only those of 12 years and over could compete. This picture shows the 'line-up' of the younger boys in 1938.

Boys Race
Steyning Walking Race. 1938.

Wartime

84.   Cavalry in Sheep Pen Lane, Steyning, *c.*1910.

85.   Brotherwood Hall decked with bunting, probably on the occasion of the peace celebrations held in the town in 1919. The building was originally the Guild Hall of the Fraternity of the Holy Trinity, hence its name. The central brick porch is dated 1614, but was altered in the 19th century.

STEYNING & DISTRICT PEACE CELEBRATION. 1919.

86.   Peace celebration in Steyning, 1919.

87.   Members of the general public from Steyning, Bramber and Beeding at their Armistice Service on 15 November 1925. Between World Wars One and Two these services were often held on the Sunday nearest to 11 November, the date on which hostilities ceased. At all times a two-minute silence was observed, in honour of the fallen.

88.   The 209th Field Company Royal Engineers (Territorial Division) on Steyning station, July 1939. The 'Terriers', as they were known, were called up for duty prior to the commencement of World War Two on 3 September 1939.

89.   Mobilisation for World War Two – No. 3 Steyning Section of the Royal Engineers outside Barclays Bank, 1939.

90. Air raid precaution exercise during World War Two, c.1943. At about this time, houses just out of sight to the left of this picture were destroyed by bombs. Note the utilitarian pram in the background. These models were produced during the war years when metal was a scarce commodity.

V-DAY

SATURDAY, 8th JUNE, 1946.

❧

Victory Celebrations

at

Steyning.

❧

PROGRAMME . . . 2d.

91. V-Day celebrations at Steyning. While these were less sophisticated than the festivities held 11 years earlier to celebrate the Silver Jubilee of the Coronation of H.M. King George V and Queen Mary, they followed a similar pattern, with the addition of a baby show, side shows, pony rides and a tea cup reading by Madame Una.

Special Occasions

92. A cause for celebration in the town was Queen Victoria's Golden Jubilee in 1887.

93. Earlier this century, life was simpler and people found entertainment in parades and meetings, many of them held in aid of charity. The members of various Friendly Societies seen in this photograph may well have attended church before processing through the town with their banners.

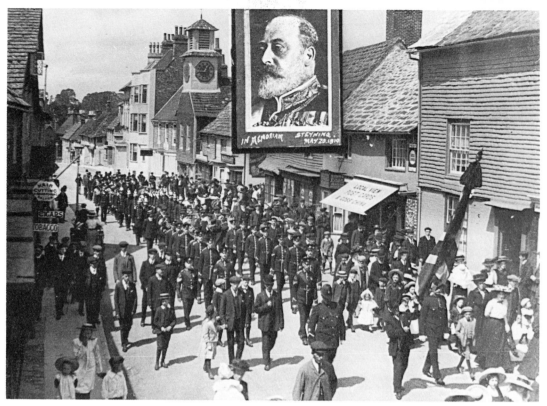

94.   Procession in the High Street in memory of King Edward VII who died in 1910.

95.   Outside the *George Inn* on a day of national mourning, probably for King Edward VII. This building is now a private house. At one time Steyning had 14 public houses.

96. An inter-denominational memorial service was held in honour of King Edward VII in St Andrew's church. Members of all local organisations took part, together with the general public. In the background are Old Malthouse Cottages, built on the site of Michell's Malthouse in Church Street. These cottages were destroyed by enemy action during World War Two.

97. Steyning has always been a popular venue for film-making. In 1920 Progress Films of Shoreham-on-Sea produced Thomas Hardy's *The Mayor of Casterbridge* and during the making of this film the police closed the High Street for the film makers. In 1924 another film was in production and this picture shows two figures on horseback, Prince Charles (later Charles II) and possibly Colonel George Gounter, in Church Street. Following his defeat at the Battle of Worcester in September 1651, Charles was forced to flee to France. Travelling in disguise, he had to cross the river Adur in order to reach the sea. He is reputed to have hidden at St Mary's, Bramber.

98. Carnival time at Steyning, 1929. From left to right, Percy Gray who was a draper, Dennis West, a printer, Lewis Wood (the only surviving member of the group), M. Holder, the station master, Teddy Holmes *behind* , a coalmerchant and haulage contractor, Frank Duke from the well-known Steyning building firm, Mr. Linfield from nearby Bramber, Handley Ham, a retired churchwarden, and Kibble White, the headmaster of the National School. Unfortunately it has been impossible to identify any of the children shown in the picture.

r the Froy

NO 20

CARNIVALL 1929.

Bramber

Despite their close proximity the histories of Bramber and Steyning have been widely divergent. Steyning was known to the Saxons, while Bramber was primarily a Norman foundation. The Battle Abbey Chronicles show that Bramber existed before Domesday but, being a late development, it did not figure in that compilation. The hill on which stands the ruined castle of Bramber must have offered a strategic site to early man, yet there is no archaeological evidence for its occupation before the Norman period. Even the Romans are believed to have disregarded this valuable prominence, commanding as it does much of the River Adur estuary.

The name Bramber is thought to mean a 'bramble thicket'. At one time it was also the name of the mainstream of 'the Bremre' or Bramber river, today the Adur. William de Braose built his castle in Bramber in about 1073 and founded a borough beneath its walls which was seen as a rival to Fécamp Abbey's borough at nearby Steyning. From its earliest history, the castle served as the centre of administration in the rape and for a time was known as 'Steyning Castle'. It stood on a knoll approximately 120 feet above the river. It is thought that the church built beneath its walls first served as a chapel for the castle rather than for the port of Bramber below. Built of knapped flints and pebbles, part of the encircling wall may still be traced today. The domestic apartments and storerooms situated beside the base of the mound can also be seen. The most significant part standing is a wall of the keep, looking like a giant monolith 76 feet high and dominating both the church and village of Bramber.

During the war between King John and the Barons the castle played an important role. The king seized both castle and estates of the third William de Braose in 1212, taking his wife and children prisoner. They are reputed to have been starved to death while in captivity. De Braose and his eldest son escaped to France, where the former died within a year (*The Book of St Mary's and the National Butterfly Museum*). It was at this time that the castle passed into the hands of 'a succession of royal henchmen'. The king himself may have occupied it, carrying out extensive repairs during the years 1212-15. It has been stated that Reginald de Braose ultimately obtained restitution of all his property from King Henry III. By the time of the Mowbray's occupation the castle ceased to be regularly inhabited; however, it did continue to serve in its administrative capacity, the honor court being held there until the 14th century. Bramber Castle housed one of the earliest mints and during the Middle Ages it became a prison. The castle was briefly occupied by parliamentary forces during the Civil War, then passed into the hands of the Royalists, before being re-taken by the Parliamentarians.

Throughout the centuries much of the stone has been carried away for other building purposes. The grounds have been put to a variety of uses. As early as the 15th century they were used for grazing, subsequently being converted into a rabbit warren. By the mid-19th century they became a favourite place for picnics, and special excursion trains were run from the coast to Bramber. Later in the century they were pleasure grounds with a fairground, swing-boats, miniature railway and tea-gardens for the visitors' entertainment before ultimately becoming, with the castle, the property of the National Trust in whose hands they remain today.

No evidence exists for a pre-Conquest crossing of the river at Bramber, though earlier ones may have existed between King's Barn and Beeding church, and perhaps another at Annington, which later became known as St Botolph's. There may have been a bridge close to the church there (*de Veteri Ponti*). Dr. Hudson feels the crossing may have been a causeway or a ford.

There is a charter dating between 1180 and 1204 confirming Sir William de Braose's earlier gift to Sele Priory of 'all his bridge of Brembre', whereas a later charter *c.*1230 refers to 'two bridges'. It is known that an agreement of 1103 refers to a bridge where a toll was paid to de Braose by ships passing through to Steyning. By 1230 there is the first definite reference to the existence of the 'greater bridge of Bramber', two bridges thus being recorded. It is thought that a splendid stone bridge was erected over the mainstream of the river, possibly during the 1180s, and a causeway or highway connected the two bridges. The lesser structure over the eastern stream may have been originally of wood, while the western bridge was built in stone. The latter had four arches, was 170ft. long and 17ft. wide with triangular recesses in which pedestrians took refuge when traffic over the bridge was heavy. It was situated close to St Mary's, and relics of the bridge were discovered in 1839 when the road was rebuilt. It is thought that on the large central pier was a chapel dedicated to St Mary, as the Monks of Sele Priory were charged with the duty to perform divine service at the Chapel on the Bridge. In 1468, the bridge was in a bad state of repair and John, Bishop of Chichester, granted an Indulgence 'to all persons in his Diocese who shall contribute to the repair of the bridge at Bramber', but this apparently had little effect as by 1473 both the bridge and the chapel were stated to be falling into decay. By 1627 the western channel was reduced to a tiny stream by the inning (reclamation) of the marshes and the silting of the estuary, and the great stone bridge became buried. (The information in this paragraph has been taken from an article by E. W. Holden in Vol. 113 of *Sussex Archaeological Collections* entitled 'New Evidence relating to Bramber Bridge'.)

The eastern bridge of timber was repaired in 1570. It had passed, along with Sele Priory, into the hands of Magdalen College, Oxford, which continued to own it until 1840. Its upkeep was apparently the responsibility of the vicar of Beeding, and it was repaired at his expense as late as the 18th century. Later in that century it was rebuilt in brick, while this century an openwork steel footbridge was built alongside. Certain confusion has arisen in the past as it was sometimes known as 'the great bridge' while postcards produced during this century refer to it variously as 'Bramber' or 'Beeding' bridge.

The embanking of the eastern course of the river some time before the 16th century led to a further reduction in the water of the western channel. Today it is a minor stream running under the main road between Bramber and Upper Beeding close to the site of St Mary's.

Bramber differs from the five other Sussex rapes in that its lordship was not the same as that of its chief town, Steyning. According to Hudson this division of lordship inevitably caused friction. Braose, unhappy at Fécamp's power in Steyning, founded a college of secular canons at his castle and endowed this college with land, tithes and other revenues in his rape.

Braose was also accused of interfering with shipping on the way to Steyning by charging the men of Fécamp Abbey a toll at his bridge. Various other encroachments were made by the Braose family including the seizure of 18 burgages in Steyning town. A royal decree of

1103 allowed a member of the Braose family to hold these burgages albeit as tenements of Steyning borough. Dr. T. P. Hudson believed that these properties were the site of houses which lay in the eastern angle between Church Street and High Street, Steyning, and came to be attached to Bramber instead of the former town for electoral and probably also for local government purposes in the 19th century.

Braose was granted a half share of Steyning's Saturday market toll by a decree dated 1086 which he and his descendants continued to claim until the 15th century. Bramber had its own market by about 1073. It is believed that the site was south-west of the castle at the junction of the village with the two old roads from Steyning. It did not thrive and by the 16th century had lapsed. Budgen's Map of Sussex 1779 mentions a 'disused market'. Braose was also granted two three-day fairs during the year, but these likewise ceased operating sometime during the 15th century.

The area covered by the castle was much greater originally than today. The medieval east-west route from Southampton to Canterbury which passed through Bramber may well have been through the castle grounds. The hamlet was also served by a wharf, which must have been used to transport material needed in the building of the castle. The 11th- and 12th-century remains of a wharf have been found in the vicinity of St Mary's. The wharf was subsequently used for the export of wealden timber. Hudson writes, 'In the mid-13th century the port seems to have been busy, timber, oak bark and faggots being loaded there. In 1322 it was among the Sussex ports ordered to supply the royal army in the north'. This port was still operating in the 14th century, but like Steyning it declined in importance with the growth of another at New Shoreham. At this time Bramber was described as 'impoverished with no merchants or tradesmen of any substance'. Apparently this situation changed little as by the 18th century Defoe noted 'that not many of the inhabitants were above asking alms from travellers'.

The earliest church to serve the castle is thought to have been a wooden structure, while the present stone one, begun in 1073, served as a chapel. Later in its history it came to be used by the castle inmates and the commonfolk alike. In 1530 the benefice was united with St Botolph's for ecclesiastical purposes. The rectory is first mentioned in the Chichester Registry of 1636 and the later schoolhouse and school were built on the same site. The earliest rectory may have suffered damage during the Civil War when a part of the church and castle were destroyed. (*Bramber and Steyning* by John G. Garratt.)

The Quakers were active in Beeding during the 17th century though no meeting house has been recorded. During the previous century, though, the church of St Nicholas had two Puritan incumbents, while two subsequent rectors were absentees.

Much of Bramber was destroyed by fire in 1286, the only house left standing being St Mary's, at that time owned by the Knights Templar. Many of the properties standing today were built during the 19th and 20th centuries, but some earlier ones date back to the 15th century. It is believed that the first houses would have been west of St Mary's between that and the castle and would have been on the site of the causeway originally occupied by the salt-workers at the nearby pans. Building stone was certainly removed from the castle for the construction of many of the later houses. The borough of Bramber appears to have been fragmented with some properties in Steyning and other urban ones belonging to the once powerful Sele Priory.

St Mary's is considered to be one of the most ancient and noteworthy houses of its kind in England. Its foundations date back to the 12th century. When Philip, Lord of Bramber, died in 1125, his widow, the Lady Aanor presented to the Knights Templar five acres of land. An early map apparently confirms this as the site on which St Mary's now stands.

The original house, sometimes called 'The Chapel or Chapter House', is thought to have been built *c.*1154, when the Templars were granted the nearby church of Sompting. St Mary's was both a residence for the monks of Sele Priory and a monastic inn for travellers on the west-east pilgrimage route between Winchester and Canterbury. Sele Priory fell into disrepute at the dissolution of the alien priories and, as a consequence, some time before 1459 the link between the priory and its parent monastery in Anjou was dissolved and it became annexed to the newly-founded College of St Mary Magdalen, Oxford. During this period St Mary's was much enlarged and redesigned on a grand scale, probably by William of Waynflete, Bishop of Winchester and founder of Magdalen College. The house, today considered to be one of the best examples of a timber-framed building of the 15th century, was originally built as a four-sided galleried inn around a courtyard, from which external staircases led to the upper rooms. A few fragments of the original building survive to this day. The chimney stacks were added during the Tudor period.

At one time the monks of Sele were 'much condemned for riotous behaviour' and the house appears to have degenerated into a noisy inn frequented by pimps and whores. At this time the western wing is believed to have been destroyed by a fire; however, one of the medieval windows survived and, known as a 'shutting-window', may still be seen in the house today.

At the time of the dissolution of the monasteries by King Henry VIII in 1539 St Mary's was granted to Francis Shirley of West Grinstead. His descendant, Thomas Shirley, built Wiston House near Steyning. Queen Elizabeth I is reputed to have visited St Mary's rather than the grander Wiston House. The painted room may have been decorated in her honour by an itinerant 'painter-stainer'. The 16th-century painting on the fireplace lintel depicts Henry VIII's warships engaging the French Armada of 1545. The *Mary Rose* was on her way to join this battle when she sank.

St Mary's had meanwhile passed out of the hands of the Shirleys into those of the Gough (later Gough-Calthorpe) family. The house was apparently much altered during the time it belonged to the Goughs. Within St Mary's is a room known as 'the King's Room', for Prince Charles (later Charles II) is reputed to have rested there before proceeding to Brighton, during his flight from the Roundheads following the Battle of Worcester in 1651. He later caught a boat at Shoreham which took him to Europe and safety.

Finally, in 1860, after nearly 300 years of family ownership, Frederick, fourth Baron Calthorpe, sold St Mary's to Richard Hudson, verger and farmer of Bramber, who was able to buy the somewhat dilapidated building for £300. In 1896 the Hon. Algernon Bourke, son of the Earl of Mayo, bought and restored it, converting the barn to a music room. However, a source of irritation to Bourke was the 'right-of-way' to St Botolph's church which passed directly under his window. Rather than fight this restriction he sold the property to Albert Musgrave in 1903. He pleased everyone by building a new road and bridge, moving the 'right-of-way' to its present position. It was at this time that A. Conan Doyle, while a visitor to the house, wrote his mystery story entitled *The Musgrave Ritual*, in which he refers to two elm trees and a secret staircase.

During the Edwardian period the house resounded with nobility, but the Great War of 1914-18 brought an end to this opulent era and the house suffered from absentee ownership, while the grounds became one of Bramber's flourishing tea-gardens. At the outbreak of World War Two St Mary's became headquarters for 150 soldiers, Canadian troops being stationed there in 1941.

St Mary's gradually declined and was threatened with demolition. However, Dorothy Ellis saved it from destruction and embarked upon a new and vital phase in the restoration of this remarkable old house. Bourke's Victorian wing was cut off and divided into flats, and a large part of the grounds was sacrificed to a caravan park. After a period of 35 years under Dorothy Ellis' ownership, when she ran it both as a guest house and antiques showroom, the house for a time became a Butterfly Museum, until January 1985, when Peter Thorogood, poet, musician, and authority on the life and work of the 19th-century comic poet and engraver, Thomas Hood, joined the long line of owners of St Mary's. Today St Mary's has been justly described as a building of 'unusual quality and haunting beauty', open to the public after extensive restoration work sympathetically carried out by the new owner, ably assisted by his artistic curator, Roger Linton.

One of the earliest industries recorded in Bramber was that of salt-panning. There were pans on the land south of the present High Street, which Garratt explains were variously referred to as the 'Salt Wates' (1602), 'Saltcoates' (1658) and the 'Salt slips' (1699). The only trade continuously recorded in Bramber was that of wheelwright. One of the medieval trades was that of ripier, or fresh fish carrier, indicating that the river was of prime importance as the source of a major part of the diet of a Catholic people.

With the coming of the railway in 1861, tourism became an important provider of employment. Day excursions by railway were run to Bramber and tea-rooms and gardens opened to cope with this expanding trade. The railway was also valuable in that it enabled the many local farmers to get their produce not only to the inland towns but also to the expanding coastal resorts.

As early as the 15th century Bramber had two inns. One was called the *White Lion* though its name was changed in the 19th century to the *Castle Hotel*. This inn was used for a variety of purposes: 'In the absence of a town hall it served for holding borough courts and elections of members of parliament' (Hudson). In spite of a small population Bramber returned members to Parliament and 'from 1295 to 1399 the borough and Steyning were represented at roughly two parliaments in three. Generally they sent two members jointly, but sometimes one or other borough sent both. From 1399 to 1453 they were not represented, but after 1453 each sent two members' (*Victoria County History*). Bribery and corruption was rife and Defoe in 1724 described elections at Bramber as scandalously mercenary. However, tradition has it that the keeper of Bramber turnpike gate was offered and refused £1,000 for his vote. The earlier nominees were normally chosen by the dukes of Norfolk, but from the 17th century Bramber returned members from two local families and the borough was consequently split between these rival factions. The Gough family was the more successful and they or their nominees sat for the borough between 1714 and 1768, except for a limited time when their interest was leased to Thomas, Lord Archer. Perhaps the borough's most illustrious member was William Wilberforce, related to the Gough family by marriage. He only visited Bramber once and, passing through the hamlet, enquired its name. On hearing it he exclaimed, 'Why that's the place I'm Member for'. The disfranchisement of this 'rotten borough' came about under the 1832 Reform Act.

The first recorded schoolmaster in Bramber was in 1592, and in 1667 the rector was licensed to teach. Subsequent schools were started by the Duke of Rutland and Lord Calthorpe early in the 19th century. This school apparently had seven pupils during the summer term but during the winter months the number doubled, due no doubt to the fact that most young children were expected to help their families on the land, especially at harvest time. Later in the century there was only a dame school, until 1858 when the

Church of England built its own school, south of St Nicholas (today a private house). The school closed in 1913 when the remaining pupils were transferred to Beeding.

The population of Bramber has always been low, but there was some increase during the 17th century. By 1801, however, the population of the parish was only 91. It fluctuated during the 19th century, peaking with the building of the railway, but by 1901 had again fallen. During the present century it has increased steadily but many of the inhabitants work outside the area.

Described as a place of tourism early in this century, what is Bramber today? The castle still stands in its ruined state overshadowing the village street. The house of St Mary's, little altered over the centuries, is a favourite place for visitors. The great bridge has disappeared beneath the road, but the causeway road remains, with the houses (with few exceptions) looking remarkably as they did nearly a century ago.

99. A bird's-eye view of Bramber village, c.1920.

100. The church of St Nicholas at Bramber was originally built as a chapel to the castle. The building has shared in the general decline of Bramber and also suffered considerable damage during the Civil War period, particularly in 1643 when Bramber Castle was destroyed and the east end of the church partially devastated. This picture by S. Hooper, dated 1785, shows the ruined church. The tower was not rebuilt until about 1790.

101. St Nicholas's church, showing the restored tower, from a drawing by H. Gastineau, c.1850.

102. Reconstruction of Bramber Castle in the Norman period, based on an old drawing. Bramber stood on a knoll approximately 120 feet above the river Adur, while the artificial mound in its centre rose a further 40 feet. During the 17th-century Civil War, the castle was alternately taken by Royalists and Parliamentarians, and around this time ceased to be a residence. Today it is but a ruin, with the surviving wall of the keep dominating the church and village beneath.

103. The figures in the foreground of this photograph, taken c.1900, give some idea of the size of the remaining wall of the keep.

104. Children in a waggonette, which must have been intended to be pulled by a horse or donkey, in the grounds of Bramber Castle, *c.*1900.

105. Conjectural drawing of Bramber bridge with the castle in the background and the chapel of St Mary on the central arch.

106. This bridge has variously been known as Bramber and as Beeding bridge. Originally it was the lesser of the two bridges which spanned the river, but today it is the only one and crosses the Adur at Beeding. The building on the left of the photograph was, prior to 1870, Bramber school. In 1926 an openwork steel footbridge was built alongside the bridge.

107. St Mary's, c.1860. At this time the house was occupied by a local farmer, Richard Hudson. The internal staircase was divided and one part served the family while the smaller section of the house was used as a labourer's cottage.

108. One of the earliest photographs of St Mary's, c.1860, when it was run as a farm. The building on the left was a barn; during the occupation of the Hon. Algernon Bourke, a music room was built on this site.

109. St Mary's early this century. In 1903 the house was sold to Albert Musgrave and the famous writer Sir Arthur Conan Doyle often stayed there. He is reputed to have written *The Musgrave Ritual* with St Mary's in mind. The two elms shown in the picture are mentioned, together with the secret stairway and underground passage.

110.   The music room was added by the Hon. Algernon Bourke when he bought St Mary's in 1896. The two medieval carved stone fireplaces, a feature of the room, were originally traceried heads to inset wall tombs from a Venetian church. This photograph was taken *c*.1914.

111. Canadian troops were stationed at St Mary's during World War Two. This photograph shows them outside the house in 1941. Following the cessation of hostilities, the building was found to be in a very bad state and there was talk of demolition.

112. Bramber village, with the castle in the background, from an early print, *c*.1840. On the left can be seen the wall of St Mary's with Priory Cottage centre right.

113. One of the earliest photographs of Bramber in existence, taken *c.*1865. On the left may be seen the toll-gates.

114. The toll-gate at Bramber from a painting, *c.*1860.

TUB RACE AT BRAMBER
FEB 2ND 1904
NAMES OF COMPETITORS AND THEIR CRAFTS
MR. H. JOYES ... "PALADIN"
" G. WINZAR ... "TADPOLE"
" G. ROSE ... "SAUCY SAL"
" E. DREWETT ... "EVANGELINE"
" B. GOOTE ... "STEAM ENGINE"
" B. CHAPMAN ... "DIAMOND JUBILEE"
" W. WATSON ... "WET HORSE"
" H. SLAUGHTER ... "CALAMITY JANE"
PALADIN SPRINGS A LEAK

115.   This is believed to be one of the earliest of the tub races, now an annual feature on the River Adur, popular with residents and visitors alike. This particular event appears to be taking place on the flooded road rather than on the river, but the competitor is using an actual tub. Today a variety of crafts are used.

116.   *Castle Hotel*, 1904. This building with its 19th-century façade is thought originally to have been the *White Lion*. At various times the building has served as a court house and all public meetings, including the election of Members of Parliament, were held there.

117.   Two horse-drawn vehicles attempting to pass one another during the winter floods of 1911. This part of the road frequently flooded and later the possibility of calling in specialists from Holland to help with the problem was considered.

118.   Bramber village was practically cut off during the disastrous floods of 1924-5 and deliveries of food had to be made by boat before the water abated. Many residents had to live in the upper storeys of their homes as the ground floors were flooded.

119. Frank Lucas (wearing the cap) and Harry Adams taking provisions to Mr. Bacon at his upper floor window during the floods in Bramber in 1925.

120. A photograph thought to be of Mr. Walter Potter outside his Museum of Curiosity at Bramber. Potter collected and stuffed many small animals and birds which he eventually housed in this museum. He created complete tableaux depicting various well-known nursery rhymes, such as the Death and Burial of Cock Robin. He also immortalised a cricket match between Steyning and Horsham, the players being stuffed guinea pigs. There were various animal freaks on exhibition, including one of a two-headed calf. Visitors came from far and wide to view these curiosities. For many years Potter's son Edgar ran this museum but unfortunately it was closed following his death.

121. These people walking along Bramber High Street, c.1900, may have arrived on an excursion train. There were many attractions at this time for visitors – the fairground and tea gardens at the Castle, Potter's Museum of Curiosities and the pleasure of trips on the river.

122. The River Adur was used both for pleasure craft and for the barges which transported clay from the pits at Horton to the cement works. The boys sitting on the bank may have been Ted and Fred Elms whose sister was the local school teacher. On the right of the bridge is a small building, formerly used as a school. This photograph was taken *c*.1905.

123. One of the many tea gardens which flourished in Bramber during the earlier years of the century, photographed *c*.1925.

124.   The horse belonging to the Castle Laundry of Bramber being shod, *c.*1908. The cart may well have been made by the Woolgars of Steyning as similar designs appeared in their pattern books. The blacksmith may have combined his work with that of wheelwright, judging by the metal rims resting against the building.

125.   Bramber High Street looking east, *c.*1920. Note the state of the road.

Beeding

Upper and Lower Beeding formed one parish until modern times, despite being some fifteen miles apart. A. Mawer and F. M. Stenton in *The Place Names of Sussex* suggest that 'Upper' may be likened to 'High' (as in High Street) to denote the most important part of the parish. An alternative explanation is that 'Upper' is the downland village and 'Lower' is in the Weald.

Throughout the centuries there have been variations in the spelling of the name, Beadingum *c.*880, Bedinges 1073, Beddinges at the time of Domesday, Bydyng 1330 and Beden in 1727. The name is thought to derive from the people of the Beada or, according to Keith Nethercoate-Bryant, from Bieda, recorded in the 'Anglo Saxon Chronicle' as a son of Port who came to this land in A.D. 501.

Prior to the Conquest, King Edward the Confessor held Beeding as a royal manor. By the time of the Domesday Survey it was divided between William de Braose, who was granted the rape of Bramber in about 1073, and William de Warenne of the rape of Lewes.

The earliest settlement may have been close to the present church of St Peter's, pieces of Roman tile having been found near there. Subsequently it became the site of the Priory of Sele and the early history of Beeding is really that of the priory, for it owned all the land in the area, including valuable salterns. The Chartulary of Sele is a profitable source of information about many of the early inhabitants (Garratt).

In about 1096 Bramber college (founded by William de Braose) was dissolved and its endowments transferred to a new foundation, the Priory of St Peter at Beeding. It came under the control of the Benedictine monastery of St Florent at Saumur. In time it overshadowed Steyning college as the chief religious foundation in the rape, but being an 'alien' house it suffered from the vicissitudes of the wars with France.

The priory is thought to have been a small house, comprising no more than six monks and a prior, together with their servants, but the Benedictines had the reputation of being energetic both in religious and temporal affairs. The monks of Sele Priory may have been responsible for the education of the younger sons of the Norman nobility living in the locality. The present church of St Peter's was the original monastic church. The cloisters of the priory were joined to the north wall of the nave of St Peter's. At the time of Domesday two churches were recorded but no trace of a second has been found – it was probably a wooden structure which fell into ruin on completion of the priory church.

The first prior, Robert, was appointed in about 1086 and much of the building work may have been carried out durng his term of office. For nearly 200 years the parish church and priory church were one, but the inhabitants had little responsibility for the running of it. However, by the 13th century, a vicar was installed with his own small house, described in a 17th-century deed as a 'little Vicaredge [sic] House in which a man cannot stand upright with a little garden and a little Henplot not half a roode of ground' (Garratt). With the coming of their own vicar, the parishioners became responsible for the nave of the church, the belfry and the bellropes, while the priory remained liable for the maintenance of the chancel. Even as early as 1283 Beeding church had been the subject of an order for repair. In 1308 major rebuilding took place, the church was extended and rededicated to SS Peter and Paul.

Throughout much of its early history the priory appeared to be in contention with various bodies, including the Knights Templar with whom they clashed in 1180 over their oratory at New Shoreham, which had been built on land belonging to Sele. Other disputes involved the collection of tithes. Sele Priory suffered much financial distress and in 1255 paid the King a tenth of all its possessions.

In the 15th century monastic life in Sussex was in decline and the link between priory and its parent monastery was dissolved. It was disposed of to Waynflete, Bishop of Winchester, for the benefit of the newly-founded Magdalen College at Oxford. However, the resident prior refused to give up his office in spite of a Bull commanding this. The eviction of the Benedictines finally took effect two years later. In 1493 the Carmelites were allowed to take possession of the buildings. Previously they had had a House at Shoreham but this had been inundated by the sea. They stayed until the dissolution of the monasteries in the reign of Henry VIII. According to Garratt, when they left, little of value remained except for the choir stalls, a bell and a few sorry vestments. By 1790 the monastic buildings were obliterated. The name is perpetuated in Priory House built as a residence for the vicars. It is believed that the graves of the monks lie under what is now the lawn at the rear of this property.

Magdalen College became responsible for the maintenance of the chancel of the church and also had the duty of presenting vicars to the living and of providing a stipend for them. This they continued to do until the mid-1950s. Consequently many of the vicars were former Fellows of Magdalen, the most famous being Owen Oglethorpe, vicar from 1531-36, who as Bishop of Carlisle crowned Queen Elizabeth I in 1559, all the other bishops having refused. (This information comes from the guidebook to the Church and Priory of St Peter's, Beeding.) In 1897 the parish was linked with Bramber, so the vicar of Beeding was the rector of Bramber. This parish included Botolph's.

The school in Beeding was one of the earliest of the church schools in the county. Aiming to educate the poorer classes, its founder was the vicar, Dr. John Rouse Bloxam, who naturally placed an emphasis on the teaching of religious knowledge. According to K. Nethercoate-Bryant, the school log book makes very interesting reading. The first entry, dated 19 March 1872, states: 'The Reverend Dr. Bloxam came into school in the afternoon and took the first class in Scripture, 64 were present in the school'. The ground on which this school stood belonged to Magdalen College: hence the tradition of education begun by the monks of Sele Priory was carried on into the present century.

Other schools have been recorded in Beeding, including one which was listed as a combined workshop and school. The 1841 census records another in the High Street. 'Richard Goddard is named as the schoolmaster with ten pupils, Charles Warner is named as a teacher aged 15.' (Nethercoate-Bryant.) This must have been one of the small boarding schools which flourished at that time. One school known as Beeding Academy was primarily an evening school during the winter months for working boys. It may have had similar aims to the Mechanics' Institutes which were founded during the 19th century, where the poorer classes could improve their chances of learning trades and crafts.

The River Adur must always have played an important part in the life of the inhabitants of Beeding. St Peter's was known as the 'River Beeding Church' and many of the itinerant barge owners went there to have their children baptised. The earliest mill would probably have been a watermill, but a windmill is shown on Budgen's map of 1724. The Nonae Return of 1342 records that 'there are no merchants or other persons except as live by the cultivation of their lands', and tradesmen are not recorded until 1636. In that year Richard Meade was named as a tavern-keeper, presumably at the *King's Head*. According to John Garratt, by the 19th century there was a wide range of trades including a dealer in marine stores, a railway ganger and a constable. As the village was at the heart of a thriving farming community it was well served by wheelwrights and blacksmiths into this century. No record exists of a market, the nearest ones being at Bramber and Steyning.

One of the earliest crops grown locally is thought to have been flax and hemp in the late 11th century, and there is an area of land in Beeding called the 'Flaxlands'. The early salterns subsequently became good marshland grazing, while sheep were to be found on the slopes of the South Downs. According to Hudson, the crops grown in this area in the early 14th century would have been barley, vetch, apples, and hemp; honey was also produced. Arable farming flourished at this time. However, with the growth of the coastal resorts of Brighton and Worthing, an improved road network, and the opening of the railway linking the farming community with these resorts, dairy farming became popular.

In 1651 the Parliamentary Survey showed that the rent of Beeding was much higher than any of the neighbouring hamlets and it was at this time that many of the present houses lining the High Street were either built or rebuilt. With this migration away from the locality of the church, it became isolated from the rest of the village.

From the 18th century, expansion took place and the road from Horsham to Beeding was made a turnpike. According to Garratt: 'In 1765 the roads were widened in view of the heavy increase in horse-drawn traffic; in 1788 and onwards the draining of the lowlands and embanking of the roads led to it eventually (1793) becoming a turnpike road and in 1805 the coaching road over the downs was enlarged'. The latter was the road from Brighton which came into the village by 'Bramber Gorge' (today's Beeding Bostal). The present road to Shoreham, which follows the river, was also turnpiked in 1807. Both Bramber and Beeding had their own toll-gates (at opposite ends of the two linked villages) which were demolished towards the end of the 19th century. However the toll-house cottage at Beeding was subsequently rebuilt for the Weald and Downland Open Air Museum at Singleton. These new roads would have eased the transportation of farm produce to the coastal resort of Brighton.

The next century saw further growth in the seaside towns and Beeding later became a miniature 'dormitory' with many of its inhabitants working elsewhere. A large proportion of the present dwellings have been built within the last 80 years. One of the most notable buildings in Beeding today is 'The Towers', an imposing French château-style structure erected *c.*1880 and today a convent school.

The Blue Circle Cement works on the river south of Beeding, originally known as 'Beeding Cement Works', was the largest employer in the locality, and the company built 'Dacre Villas' to house some of their workers.

The 11th-century Domesday Survey showed the population of Beeding as 62 villagers and 48 smallholders. By 1801 this had risen to 459. Today the population of the village and surrounding area is estimated to be in the region of 5,000. A visitor walking along the length of the main street linking the two villages of Bramber and Beeding, and crossing the River Adur, would perhaps have difficulty in defining where one ended and the other began, so closely are they entwined.

Much of the information in this introduction was derived from *Bramber and Steyning* by the late John G. Garratt.

126. Beeding Priory House, built in the 18th century on the site of an earlier one, was once used as the vicarage. Today only the name survives to remind people that at one time the great Priory of Sele was established here. The graves of the monks are believed to lie under the lawn.

127. Beeding village street in 1905, with the *King's Head* public house on the right.

128.   Infants and teacher outside Beeding school, *c.*1890. The girls are wearing pinafores in order to protect their garments, while most of the boys are dressed in dark suits with white collars.

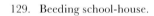

129.   Beeding school-house.

130. Upper Beeding schoolchildren in 1919, with the headmaster, Mr. Mimack. Many of these children still live in the locality today.

131. A class at Beeding school, *c.*1930. Note the old desks with their fixed seats and the lack of stimulating materials on the walls of the classroom.

132. Beeding Scout and Cub troop, *c.*1920. Many of the boys are alive today and living in the area.

133. Some boys of Beeding earlier this century. They include Gordon Chapman (second man from left, standing), then Fred Elms, Mr. Early, Charlie Penfold, Mr. Weller and, the last man on the right-hand side, Harry Woolgar. In the centre at the front is Ernie Young.

134. Beeding trap ball team. Trap ball is one of the earliest English games, going back to the 14th century, and it may be related to the primitive game of 'tip-cat'. There is some evidence of a ceremonial origin.

135. The post mill, *c*.1870, with Mr. Breech on horseback. This mill, together with cottage, stabling and outbuildings, was offered for sale in 1864.

136. Notice relating to the sale of the post windmill at Upper Beeding. The mill, at this time described as a 'grist mill', was let to Mr. Peter Wood at the very low rental of £40 per annum. The sale came about when Mr. Wood's tenancy expired in 1864. The auction took place at the *White Horse Hotel*, Steyning, on Monday 5 September 1864.

PARTICULARS.

THIS DESIRABLE

FREEHOLD PROPERTY

IS SITUATE AT

UPPER BEEDING, SUSSEX,

AND CONSISTS OF A

POST WINDMILL,

WITH

TWO PAIR OF STONES, FANTAIL, PATENT SAILS, AND ALL THE RUNNING GEAR BELONGING THERETO,

KNOWN AS

BEEDING MILL;

ALSO A

COTTAGE, STABLING, LAND, AND OUT-BUILDINGS

ADJOINING.

The above Mill is desirably situate as a Grist Mill, and is now let to Mr. Peter Wood at the low rental of £40 per annum, and whose tenancy will shortly expire.

137.   A drawing made *c*.1860 of the windmill near Upper Beeding.

138.   The delivery cart of A. J. Perry, baker and grocer of Beeding, *c*.1920.

139. Pre-1913 Humber delivery van. The 'ghost' figures on the left are Allen Steel, who was a baker, and Emily Lucas. In the vehicle are Obadiah and Mrs. Lucas with William Holman, Obadiah's stepson.

140. Beeding High Street, *c.*1915. On the right is Lucas's store.

141. The postmistress Ann Stoner with her brother (who had been a postman at one point in his life), outside 'Holly Cottage' which was the post office in Beeding, earlier this century.

142. Riverside, Upper Beeding. At one time the cottage on the right was the post office.

BEEDING CEMENT WORKS.

143. Blue Circle Industries PLC are today the owners of the cement works on the River Adur. Since the last century these works have provided occupation for many local men. Early in their history the works were used for lime burning, but in 1884 they changed ownership and became R. G. Lewis & Company. The six chamber kilns produced approximately 150 tons of cement per week. In 1896 or 1897 the Sussex Portland Cement Company of Newhaven bought out the previous owners and increased the capacity of the works considerably. The chalk required for lime burning and afterwards for cement manufacture was obtained from the quarry cut out of the Downs to the east of the road, while the clay required for cement manufacture was at first brought from the Medway by the barge *Abner*. However, the Sussex Portland Cement Company installed a railway siding and had the clay brought from Glynde, near Lewes. Later a clay pit opened at Horton, three miles north of Shoreham Works, and clay was brought down the River Adur by 20-ton barges, drawn by a small steam tug. During the early part of the century cement was conveyed to Shoreham Harbour by barge for shipment to Poole and Southampton. On the return journey coal was transported. The British Portland Cement Manufacturers took over the works in 1912 and immediately increased production. Between 1948 and 1951 complete rebuilding and modernisation took place. The early wooden bridge on the River Adur near Bramber church had central supporting piles. This prevented navigation so the Company arranged with the River Adur Trustees to find the money to replace the wooden bridge with the present iron one.

144. Cement barges being towed by a tug on the River Adur early this century.

145. Beeding men building 'Dacre Villas', home for many of the workers at Beeding Cement Works, whose chimneys can be seen in the background. The men are all carrying the tools of their trade. The man standing on the right of the picture and the seated worker with the dog were brothers, Ted and Fred Elms. Fred Elms Snr. sits next to the man who is serving refreshments. It was common practice at this time for family members to work together.

146. The public house on the right was at one time tied to the Steyning Brewery. Today it is the *Rising Sun*, Upper Beeding. Approximately halfway down on the left may be seen part of the Beeding toll on Shoreham Road. The farm buildings visible between the trees on the right belong to Beeding Court Farm. This photograph was taken *c.*1914.

147. George Bazen (second from right) with his sheep shearing team at Hoe Court Farm. The shearers normally worked in a barn or shed, the floor of which was usually swept clean before the work commenced. On large farms, where extra hands were employed at clipping time, one man was appointed to sharpen the blades of the handshears on a stone during the course of the day.

148. On 10 October 1905 Mr. and Mrs. Cross, their six sons and four daughters moved from Oathill Farm in Crewkerne, Somerset, to Beeding Court Farm. Mr. Cross was a dairy farmer and felt that milk would have a better market in West Sussex, due to the growth of the seaside towns and resorts, the nearness to London and the good railway network. This picture shows the family and several of their farm workers, including 15-year-old Alfred Parker, outside Oathill Farm. A special train was laid on for their departure,taking livestock, furniture, farm implements, domestic animals and various 'goods and chattels'. Before the train left at midnight, between 200 and 300 neighbours gathered to wish them well. This train arrived at Steyning early the next morning, and the cattle walked from the station to the farm via Bramber. In the meantime the two eldest sons, Tom and Oliver, each drove a team of horses and carts, loaded with more goods, to Sussex, breaking their long journey in Hampshire. Mr. and Mrs. Cross were active members in the Free Church and founders of the Baptist Church at Upper Beeding. For seven years services were held in the kitchen of the farmhouse.

149. Beeding Court, the farm to which the Cross family came in 1905.

150.   George Bailey, shepherd at Beeding Court Farm, with a young assistant. Note the wattle hurdles which were normally used to fold the sheep at lambing time.

151. The Towers, Upper Beeding, in the course of construction, c.1870. It was built as a folly or a shooting lodge for Mr. Smith, perhaps the gentleman on the seat. It continued as a private residence until 1903, when it became a Catholic boarding school. It is still a convent school today.

152. Two of the nuns from the convent of the Blessed Sacrament (Beeding Towers), 1909. The Lady Superior was Madame Marie Alexina Joris.

153. The 'family' at The Towers, c.1885, possibly that of Mr. George Smith who built this private folly.

154. During the Victorian era it was customary to photograph both the families and their servants, who were usually dressed in their finery. Here the maids are wearing their afternoon uniform. Watching from the window of The Towers is a member of the family.

03.

BEEDING & BRAMBER   INFAN

HALL-STEYNI...

WELFARE CLINIC 1930

155. Young mothers with their babies and older children, sitting with the nurse at the Beeding and Bramber Infant Welfare Clinic in 1930. As was the fashion at that time, nearly every mother is wearing a hat.

156. Waiting for the bride, 1909. Judging by the awning over the pathway from the road to the entrance to St Peter's church, a considerable distance, this must have been the marriage of one of the wealthier parishioners.

157. Beeding and Bramber flower show, 1913. The figure with his back to the marquee was Mr. Mimack, the headmaster of Upper Beeding school, a well-known personality of the day.

158. The fête of 1927 with competitors taking part in the 'buns and treacle' event. It is interesting to see that many of the spectators are wearing hats, as is one of the entrants.

159. Bramber and Beeding fête, held in 1927 to raise funds for the building of the Village Hall, eventually erected in 1930. The man in uniform is thought to be the village 'bobby'.

No5. BRAMBER & BEEDING F

E Sep^t 1st 1927. HALL STEYNIN

160. Entrants in the children's fancy dress competition at the Bramber and Beeding fête.

NO I.

BRAMBER +BEEDING WOME

10TH ANNIVERSARY PART

161.   Bramber and Beeding Women's Institute 10th anniversary party held on 6 June 1928.
Village functions were usually held in the field, once part of Pond Farm, which is now Dawn
Close.

HALL
STEYNING

INSTITUTE
JUNE 6 · 1928 .

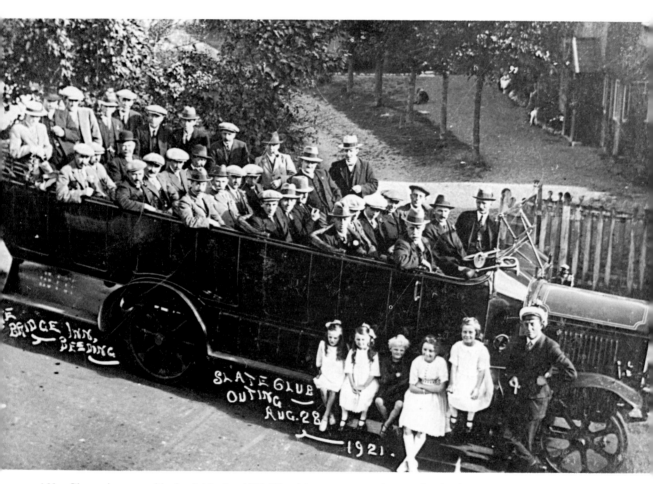

162. Char-a-banc outside the *Bridge Inn*, 1921. The driver appears to be standing beside the children on the 'running-board' which doubled as a step and was also useful for storing cans of petrol. Unfortunately it has been impossible to ascertain the destination of the Slate Club outing on 28 August – probably one of the nearby coastal resorts.

Bibliography

Armstrong, J. R., *A History of Sussex*, 1961

Baker, Michael H. C., *Sussex Villages*, 1977

Blaker, Nathaniel Paine, *Sussex in Bygone Days*, 1919

Brandon, Peter, *The Sussex Landscape*, 1974

Burke, John, *Sussex*, 1974

Butler, A. M., *Steyning Sussex*, 1928

Cleland, Jim, *The Visitors Guide to Sussex*, 1985

Cox, Ernest W. and Duke, Frank, *In and Around Steyning*, 1954

Defoe, Daniel, *Tour Through England and Wales* (Vols. 1 & 2)

Dallaway and Cartwright, *History of Western Division of Sussex* (Vols. 1 & 2)

Garratt, John G., *Bramber and Steyning*, 1973

Goodwin, John, *The Military Defence of West Sussex*, 1985

Grigg, C. A., 'Memories of Steyning'

Guy, John, *Castles in Sussex*, 1984

Ham, Joan, *Storrington in Living Memory*, 1982

Horsfield, T., *The History, Antiquities and Topography of the County of Sussex*, 1835

Kelly's Directories (Sussex)

Lower, M. A., *Worthies of Sussex*

Lowerson, John, *A Short History of Sussex*, 1980

Lowerson, John, and Myerscough, J., *Time to Spare in Victorian England*, 1977

Memories of Steyning and Sussex (Steyning Museum Trust)

Meynell, Esther, *Sussex*, 1947

Moore, Charles, *The Green Roof of Sussex*, 1984

Nairn, I., and Pevsner, N., *Sussex (Buildings of England)*, 1965

Price, Bernard, *Sussex People, Places and Things*, 1975

Recknell, G. H., *Steyning Sussex. History and Descriptive Survey*, 1965

Sleight, J. M., *A Very Exceptional Instance: Three Centuries of Education in Steyning, Sussex*, 1981

Southern History (Vol. 2) 'A Review of the History of Southern England', ed. J. R. Lowerson, 1980

Sussex County Magazine (Vols. 5, 6, 7, 10 & 27)

Turner, Howard J. T., *London, Brighton and South Coast Railways, Establishment and Growth*, 1978

Victoria County History Vol. VI Part I, ed. T. P. Hudson

Wolseley, Viscountess, *Sussex in the Past*, 1928

Woodford, Cecile, *Portrait of Sussex*, 1972

Young, Arthur, *General View of the Agriculture of Sussex* (1813).

Guide Books

Homelands Handbooks (Official Guide), 1907
Steyning Conservation Area Guide: A Pictorial Walking Trail, 1980
Ward-Lock & Co.'s Illustrated Guide Books (Series 1932-33)

Guides to the following churches were also used: St Andrew's, Steyning; St Botolph's; the Church of Coombes; St Nicholas', Bramber; St Peter's, Beeding.